Where the Sky is Born

Living in the Land of the Maya

Jeanine Lee Kitchel

Enchanted Island Press
Haiku, Hawaii

Enchanted Island Press
690 East Kuiaha Road
Haiku, HI 96708-5438 USA
www.yucatantales.com

Cover design by Karen Ross
Interior Design and Typography by Debra Lordan

Publisher's Cataloging-in-Publication

Kitchel, Jeanine Lee
    Where the sky is born: living in the land of the Maya/Jeanine
Lee Kitchel.
    p. cm.
    Includes bibliographical references.
    LCCN 2003111968
    ISBN 0-9744839-0-7

    1. Kitchel, Jeanine Lee--Travel--Mexico--Puerto Morelos. 2. Kitchel, Jeanine Lee--Travel--Yucatan Peninsula. 3. Americans--Mexico--Puerto Morelos--Biography. 4. Women booksellers--Mexico--Puerto Morelos--Biography. 5. Puerto Morelos (Mexico)--Biography. 6. Yucatan Peninsula--Description and travel. I. Title.

F1391.P917K58 2003   972'.670836'092
                            QBI03-200719

First Edition

Printed in the United States of America

Acknowledgments

Muchas gracias to Linda Boyden, Deborah Iida,
Donna Lee Gorrell, Kathy Loretta, Carole Glab,
Ron Mader for getting me started,
to the people of Mexico,
the pueblo of Puerto Morelos,
and of course,
to Paul.

Author's Note

The following is a true story, however names and places have been changed, with the exception of Ana Mario Almada and Ana Luisa Aguilar, Amar Inn, *Lu'um Ka'naab*, and *Posada Amo*r. Conversations are written as accurately as can be remembered and not intended to be exact quotations. The sequence of events in this book took place over a span of sixteen years. Most events are in chronological order, but I have condensed the timeline in some areas.

"Not all who wander are lost."

—J.R.R. Tolkien

Contents

The Umbrella

Highway 307 on Mexico's Yucatan Peninsula stretched like an asphalt ribbon before us. The Maya named this place *Sian Ka'an*, or "where the sky is born." It was untouched, this open, desolate wilderness, except for the narrow strip of pavement beneath us.

Standing there at the crossroads on the highway, more like a swath cut from the low scrub jungle than the major thoroughfare for the state of Quintana Roo, I wondered if the bus would ever come.

The year was 1985. We were sixty miles from the sparkling new resort city Cancun. It seemed unfathomable that just an hour's drive on virgin highway separated us from the traffic and noise of a city, and then, as if by sleight of hand, we were transported into a world of sky, clouds, jungle. We were in the heart of the Yucatan, land of the ancient Maya and their pyramids.

We had embarked on an extended vacation, escaping our city jobs for a few weeks to relax in the Mexican Caribbean. Another four hours south and we could be in Belize, but we had other plans that day.

After spending the night in a rustic hotel at the Tulum pyramids we planned to explore the Gulf Coast and to visit the undeveloped island Holbox near Río Lagartos. Someone had told us to catch the bus at the crossroads, where we now waited. The bus route would jog past the pyramids at Cobá and then head north through the heart of Maya land.

In a lackadaisical way, I suppose we were searching for something in this flat, wild territory that just forty years ago had been called the most savage coast in Central America. We had no idea in a few years' time we would be buying property and building a house in this foreign land. But at the moment, we were deep in the Yucatan jungle, on a sideroad to seemingly nowhere.

Paul, my fiancé, had traipsed ahead of me, carrying the bulk of our belongings on his able shoulders. Nearly six feet, he looked much younger than his forty-three years. I noticed the morning dampness had caused his sun-bleached hair to curl slightly at the ends. My own hair, light brown and shoulder-length, was well on the way to a bad hair day.

Rain was coming. Unbearable humidity and not yet 9 a.m., but this was typical weather for the neo-tropical rainforests of southern Mexico. Moments later, when the skies opened delivering a heavy downpour, we moved beneath the branches of a *Ceiba*—the Maya tree of life—for shelter. Steam began to rise slowly from the asphalt, hovering about ankle height. Still no bus.

Then rounding the corner careened a small rusty Honda. Brakes squealing, it screeched to a stop in front of us. We had no idea that our future would be determined by accepting a ride with the man who drove this car. He would lend us a yellow umbrella. It seemed a simple act at the time, but the desire to return that umbrella changed the course of our lives for it introduced us to the place we would one day call home, Puerto Morelos.

The driver, Alejandro, was in his late forties with the dark, good looks of a Castilian. He waved us over as his girlfriend, Karla, rolled down the window. She looked and dressed like an American, ten years his junior, with her brunette hair cut stylishly short. Both were smiling broadly, as if they already knew us.

"Where are you going?" he asked, barely an accent to his perfect English.

"Up to Isla Holbox, through Chemax," Paul answered. Chemax was a Mayan village forty miles north, known for its church, one of the oldest in the Yucatan.

"Well, hop in. We're going to the Cobá pyramids for the day and we can give you a lift to the crossroads."

It didn't take long to organize our things and crowd into the back seat. What a relief. Number one, we were out of the rain, soon to be mobile. Number two, the driver spoke our language. As we progressed in a westerly direction, Alejandro spoke casually about himself, where he was from, the San Francisco area like ourselves, and their day trip to the pyramids. He had the air of a storyteller, recounting tales of spider monkeys and crocodiles that lived at the pyramid site near the lake, explaining that Cobá had been one of the largest Mayan cities in the Yucatan, with over 200,000 people, although at present, only five percent of it was excavated.

The man radiated charisma, flashing comfortable smiles at Karla as he chatted easily, all the while fascinating us with his accounts of the Quintana Roo jungles. And if these tales weren't enough, hundreds of iridescent blue Morpho butterflies engulfed the car in a cloud of turquoise just then, adding a touch of Fellini, or better yet, Gabriel Garcia Marquez.

He definitely had our attention. Then he told us about the house he was building in a small fishing village called Puerto Morelos. We were intrigued.

"Where is that?" Paul asked as he tried to locate the map from his duffel bag. "We've been traveling through the Yucatan looking for smaller towns. It doesn't sound familiar."

"Puerto Morelos is twenty-five miles south of Cancun. Have you seen the Pemex station between Cancun and Tulum? The only gas station for one hundred miles?"

Even this simple statement reminded us how far from civilization we were. As Californians, it was hard to fathom one hundred miles of road without a gas station anywhere on the planet, no matter how far into the rain forest jungle one might be.

"Turn at the Pemex," Alejandro continued, "and head towards the beach. In a few minutes you'll be at the town square."

As we approached the Cobá junction, the rain continued to fall, now in a more menacing manner. Alejandro slowed to a stop at the crossroads that led to the pyramid site, his destination, or the Maya outback, ours. He fumbled beneath his seat and grabbed something. A yellow umbrella.

"Take this umbrella," he said, holding it out, bouquet fashion. "This rain won't be stopping anytime soon."

"We'll be fine. It can't last forever," I replied, not wanting to impose more on this accommodating stranger who already felt familiar to me.

"No," he insisted. "Take the umbrella."

"Only if we can return it to you," Paul interjected, apparently sensing my hesitation.

"Sure, why not? If you do, that's fine, and you can see my house. If not, don't worry about it. Directions . . . When you get to Puerto Morelos, take the first left and head all the way out the beach road. Once you pass the hotel, my house will be the first on the beach. It's Mediterranean style, you can't miss it. Who knows," he continued as we locked eyes, "maybe we'll see you later. *Hasta luego.*"

And with that, he and Karla departed. We watched them drive in the direction of the pyramids as we began walking down the wet and isolated jungle road, with forest so thick on either side of us it seemed to be on the verge of devouring the asphalt. Just two days earlier we'd seen an eighteen-wheeler hanging—or suspended—in the roadside thicket as if by velcro, all wheels well off the ground. The jungle had sucked it in when it crashed, offering a surreal resting spot. Getting it out would be another story.

As for us, we were on the road again. Time for another adventure as our path curved northwards away from the coast and inland, to Maya country.

Days later, worn out from touring various villages in the northern Yucatan and visiting Isla Holbox, we were ready to return to the calm of the coast. We were still searching for an ideal place that hadn't materialized. But the seed was planted. Maybe Puerto Morelos would be that paradise.

The Land Deal

I fell under Mexico's enchantment when I was twenty-four and living in Mendocino County, California, where I'd moved a few years after graduating from college in the midwest.

Living on the land was a novel idea then, and I wanted to try it out. After searching all summer, I found the perfect wood frame cabin in the redwoods. Just as fall approached and the air became crisp, I moved into my cottage. But I was hardly prepared for Northern California winters, especially when my new home depended on an Ashley wood stove for warmth rather than central heating. That meant firewood needed to be chopped. Talk about a change in consciousness.

My hands were calloused from chopping wood when my boyfriend called. He had just received an invitation from a surfer who had traveled to Mexico for the winter and was inviting us to join him in San Blas. All we had to do was get there. I checked it out on a Triple A map, and it looked like the perfect spot to catch some sun and surf. No worries about staying warm.

Once south of Tijuana, the twenty-four hour bus ride to Guadalajara launched me straight into the soul of Mexico, and in spite of my inadequate grasp of the language, I fell in love with the Mexican people and their culture. That winter marked an entry into an entirely new world for me, and although the boyfriend didn't last, my love affair with Mexico survived.

———>•<———

South of Cancun, the local bus dropped us at the highway near the Pemex Gas Station, and Paul and I walked the few kilometers to Puerto Morelos. Coco palms were planted in a line all the way down the narrow two lane road. Mangrove swamps with shallow brown water bumped up to the roadway, a few ducks in attendance. Lazy dragonflies hovered aimlessly at the water's edge. No cars passed us, only an ancient bike ambled by with a young rider balancing a pot of tortillas on the handle bars.

At *el centro* my first impression was that of a rustic, unpolished little *pueblo* with a few local shops. The town square, known as *el zócalo* in Spanish, lacked foliage, either by design or lack of interest, except for a large *almendron*, or almond tree, dead center and a couple of scruffy *piñones* or pines. A basketball court, though off to the side, predominated, its backboards lacking hoops and nets. Several concrete park benches donated by the town fathers lined the pathways. One or two of the benches needed repair.

Walking out towards the pier we watched pelicans dive effortlessly into the water. Fishermen, in typical Mexican fashion, brought in the day's catch, dragging fish in coolers to the well-worn dock. Just a half mile offshore waves broke on the Palancar Reef, second in size only to the Great Barrier Reef of Australia. The Palancar hugged the Mexican coast southwards one hundred and fifty miles all the way to Belize, accompanied by some of the whitest sand beaches in the world.

A crooked little lighthouse—circa who-knew-when—added cockeyed charm to the picture. The handful of locals working that day nodded to us in passing, exchanging smiles or greetings.

Friendly. No doubt about it, the place was authentic. No gringos, save us. We eavesdropped on conversations, thankful they were in Spanish. Could this be the place we'd been searching for? It had just the right amount of funk.

Giddy, we decided to ground ourselves with a bite to eat at one of the local restaurants before finding Alejandro's house. We chose one right on the beach with a large, thatched *palapa* roof. The waiter, dressed all in white, meandered over with menus and asked quietly if we would like something to drink.

"Let's drink to our good luck," Paul said. Then he ordered two margaritas.

The tone was set. Although it was early afternoon we were celebrating this occasion, finding Puerto Morelos. It seemed fitting. We both smiled, knowing we were one step closer to our shared goal. Ever since we'd met Alejandro and he'd given us the umbrella, it was as if magic was at work. Mayan magic? Here we were in the land of the ancient Maya and we were beginning to feel at home.

After a Yucateca style lunch featuring the local cuisine—fresh *camarones* with garlic for me, *pibil* chicken, a Mayan specialty with the fowl wrapped in banana leaves for Paul, and zesty lime soup—we sat for a moment on the outdoor terrace and took everything in. From the *tiburonera* fishing boats docked nearby to the rustic, neglected beach to the calm that eminated everywhere, this was certainly Mexico.

Finding the beach road was easy. Made from *sascab*, it was a lime-gravel mixture the Mayans had mined from caves and used on their roads for more than a millennium. Its density was like fine gravel, light and chalky in color, and found everywhere in the Yucatan. For at least fifteen hundred years the Mayans used these roads for a complicated system of commerce and trade. Their warring oligarchies stretched from as far north as the

Yucatan Peninsula, where we were, to southern Guatemala. The roadways were built to be used by runners who carried news back and forth.

Although we had no news to bring, we did have something to return, and we walked as briskly as we could, bearing our duffels and our talisman, the umbrella, with us.

It was mid-March and the day was hot but a slight breeze made it bearable. Low jungle lay on either side of us. As we walked, we watched small golden finches flit from tree to tree. An occasional vulture caught thermals high above us and we felt like we were far from *el centro*, although it was less than a kilometer. In a few minutes we saw a hotel, *Cabañas La Ceiba*. What a charming place it was with ten *cabanãs* on the beach and a large reception area with an attached restaurant. Hibiscus, *tulipanes* in Spanish, were everywhere—bright flowers exploding in reds and pinks. Coco palms cluttered the beach in tropical fashion. A young boy raked the sand in front of the administration desk. He paused to watch us as we walked by, and then smiled as he called out, "*Buenas tardes.*"

Next stop would be Alejandro's, and as we rounded the last curve in the road, we spotted his Mediterranean style house. With its curved walls, white trim, arched windows, and bright purple and red bougainvillea growing up the sides, it was more than we expected. I felt like Alice going through the looking glass: surely I had passed the point of no return. Could I ever go back to my office job in San Francisco after seeing life being lived this languidly, this serenely, this fully?

We walked up the beach, approached the entrance and knocked. Alejandro answered the door with a flourish and a large welcome. As he ushered us in through the handmade mahogany door, we could see straight through to the Caribbean, a shimmering turquoise blue. It felt as if we were coming home.

"Your trip? It's been good?" he asked, smiling as he took my duffel bag and waved us into a colonial style kitchen with views of the water. Paul grabbed my hand and squeezed it as we shared a glance in disbelief at this set-up.

"Of course you'll stay here for a few days, collect your thoughts, relax," he assured us, as though he were the grand tour guide of our lives. In the back of my mind I kept thinking, maybe he is.

After pleasantries were exchanged we agreed to his gracious offer—to stay as his guests, Mayan style, in this luxurious house on the beach. What luck. All this over the return of an umbrella.

While enjoying Alejandro's hospitality, I kept tossing around the budding idea—could we live here in the Yucatan? Alejandro made it seem so easy. He had built a lovely home and had been blessed with good fortune in the process. After depositing his construction money in the Puerto Morelos bank, the peso doubled in value. His original deposit soared to twice its original amount over twelve months' time. Basically, he built his home for nothing except the time he put into it.

Originally from Mexico, he had migrated to the U.S. after college and had made a name for himself on the race car circuit. Then, after a few years of racing and driving, he had settled into his life's work, architecture. He'd lived in San Francisco for the past seventeen years and had only decided to move back to Mexico when his father's health declined. As a builder and architect, buying land and developing it seemed a perfect pastime for him while he helped his mother with the family business.

And because he was a contractor at heart, with this unexpected windfall caused by the peso's surge, he decided to invest in land south of Playa del Carmen where he had purchased twenty hectares (one hectare is 2.5 acres) of beachfront property. He was opening it up to investors. Would we be interested in looking at a beachfront lot just south of Playa del Carmen?

We spent a night in Playa del Carmen in 1983 when it was little more than a Caribbean backwash, population five hundred. At that time, the town had claimed two hotels —the Blue Parrot and Hotel Lucy. Neither could be called charming; both were extremely cheap, seedy at best. We had chosen Hotel Lucy more for its raucous pink paint job than for anything else. Across the pot-holed street stood a pharmacy with a chained monkey on a stick, either as a mascot or a marketing ploy. We'd never figured out which.

In our wanderings we'd gone down to the ferry dock for Cozumel and had talked to a guy who was opening a restaurant on the beach. The town had rustic appeal, mostly because absolutely nothing was to be found there. When you reached Playa del Carmen in those days, you felt you'd reached the end of the world. It was as exciting as an afternoon siesta . . . a couple of shops, but otherwise the town barely existed. Big beaches, a few *palapas*, the rustic dock—that was Playa in 1983. No more, no less.

Now it was 1985. At some point in our travels we had become serious about buying land in Mexico; no beachfront lots were available in Puerto Morelos, and Alejandro was offering us land in Playa.

He seemed a competent contractor with much in his favor. As an architect in San Francisco he had designed several homes there plus he'd been involved in a restoration project in the East Bay. But when we honestly reviewed our prospects, we looked at the construction of his own Puerto Morelos home which said it all. The design was a unique blend of Mexicana and Mediterrano elements. He had successfully incorporated the use of local materials and workmanship into the house including rock walls, concrete niches, handmade Mexican tile, luscious hardwoods, and shell art designs in floors, walls, and on ceilings.

The house exuded the feel of a Mediterranean villa, with an enclosed interior courtyard and outdoor terraces. It could easily have been perched on the Aegean Sea rather than the Caribbean. But the height of his technique came in his use of sand and sea as backdrop. His architecture gave the illusion of bringing you indoors and out at the same time. On opening the front door, your gaze continued through a set of tandem French doors which looked out onto a white sand beach, and extended to the turquoise sea. Mesmerizing.

House concept and design aside, we also had the umbilical cord of the umbrella tying us to Alejandro. After all, would we ever have found this spot if he hadn't loaned us the umbrella that day on the Cobá road? We couldn't help but wonder how this was all transpiring. Was it fate? Whatever it was, we were hooked.

"Maybe this is what we're looking for," Paul said after we had discussed the possibility. "When can we see the property?"

"I can meet you in Playa del Carmen on Saturday. How about 1 p.m. at the small *palapa* restaurant near the dock? Then we'll drive to the land."

———————⟶►◄⟵———————

Playa del Carmen had been busy re-inventing itself since we'd last been there and a fashionable two-story hotel, *Los Mochis,* had been constructed near the ferry dock, complete with plaza. Gone was the ennui of years before. This was definitely a different Playa del Carmen. A sense of purpose now filled the air—there was money to be made. Vendors hawked their wares in true Mexican fashion. Newly thatched palm *palapas* sat on the beach tempting tourists with offerings of *cerveza* and *mariscos,* seafood appetizers. The town was experiencing a renaissance—from forgotten *pueblo* to newly discovered seaside resort. But still, Paul and I could not shake the thought that it felt like a border town. Like Chetumal, Quintana Roo's rustic state capital, but on the beach.

Playacar, an upscale housing development with a handful of spacious homes and plenty of room to grow, had also emerged. It shared the northern boundary on Alejandro's new land acquisition. Although not much was developed at the time, the size of the lots and the looks of the homes told the story: this was going to be bucks-up gringo country.

Having Playacar as a neighbor could only help, and it was clear to us that Alejandro had big plans for his killer piece of real estate. Everything was for sale with the exception of two large middle lots he was saving for himself. Were we interested in buying a beachfront lot?

"What's your asking price?" Paul questioned.

"Because you would be first tier investors, $15,000 for the beachfront lots and corner end lots are still available. You could take one of those," replied Alejandro.

We made a unanimous decision very quickly on the spot. The answer was yes. A beachfront lot! In this beautiful paradise with Alejandro as our contractor! Things were looking up, and we were one step closer to escaping city life and living our dream in Mexico.

"That's perfect," said Paul, although he later confessed he wondered where we would borrow cash for this purchase. Master card? "We'd like a corner lot. Now, how do we begin?"

On the drive back to Puerto Morelos, Alejandro explained the mystery of buying land, as a foreigner, in Mexico. Although we already had some previous knowledge of the *fideicomiso*, or real estate trust, we were happy to get a refresher course.

In 1917, the Mexican government passed a referendum which forbade foreigners from owning land closer than fifty kilometers to the ocean or its borders, Alejandro began. This took place shortly after World War I ended when Germans were on a buying spree for beachfront property.

The Mexican nationals did not want to lose their beaches to foreigners. From that point on, all foreigners were required to have a Mexican partner in land transactions. For most, the partner was a Mexico bank who held a (now) fifty year renewable trust. The fee simple title was placed in the name of the bank selected as trustee for the property owner, giving the buyer full ownership rights to buy, sell, lease the land, or pass it on to heirs.

"I'm still in the final stages myself of clearing title for my land," Alejandro continued.

"Until that is finalized, I cannot subdivide the property, but I expect it to happen within the next year."

It was April 1985. A whole year to wait for our dream land to be finalized seemed much too long. Looking at each other, we were aware of the other's thoughts.

Alejandro must have read our minds, for then he said, "Of course, we can go ahead and write up a formal contract staking out the lot you plan to buy. We'll draw it up and notarize it, and once my title has cleared, you will be ready to build. We can transfer funds at the time we draw up the contract. Then you will be ready to have your *fideicomiso* prepared."

This seemed the appropriate way to move forward. As Alejandro planned to be in San Francisco in a couple months, we decided to have the contract for the property drawn up at that time. We shook hands on the deal, and I smiled inwardly at our good luck.

As we still had a few more days' vacation time, we decided to rent a bungalow at *Cabañas La Ceiba* next to Alejandro's and settle into the solitude of the local beaches. At night we walked into town along the dark jungle road, slowly becoming accustomed to finding our way without the aid of a flashlight, guided only by the rays of the moon. In Puerto Morelos we were getting used to the streets, the people, the tempo of life. We knew when to find the bank open; what day the vegetable vendor set up his stand; what time we could find the sporadic baker selling bread.

We noticed the friendliness of everyone from children playing in the street to taxi drivers to shopkeepers. We started to become accustomed to the polite nods or the occasional *"buenas tardes"* from people we didn't even know. We were fitting in.

In town, the streets weren't complete without an ensemble of scrawny, aimless dogs sleeping in the sweltering sun. We called them throwbacks, dingo dogs, for their wild, untamed looks. They weren't vicious, nor did they bark; they just slept in the streets undisturbed. Even when the occasional car came close to hitting them, they barely moved.

To us, this epitomized Puerto Morelos: life was so secure, dogs could comfortably sleep in the street uninhibited and unconcerned. That was when we nicknamed Puerto Morelos "Town of Dogs."

The Waiting Game

Back in San Francisco we returned to life as we knew it: work, stress and traffic. I'd been living in San Francisco since 1980 having decided to try city life after my back-to-the-land days. By this time, I was in my thirties and had learned to conceal my free spirit and rebellious nature and worked as a sales representative for a large commercial printer. A friend set me up with the job. She was making a six-figure income with this company on a straight commission basis, and her customer base was the high-tech electronics firms then emerging in Silicon Valley.

On applying for the position I felt I was selling out by not using my journalism degree, but after canvassing all my women friends, I realized she was the only woman I knew who enjoyed her work and was well paid for her efforts. The rest of us seemed stuck in dead-end, low-paying mid-management jobs.

Having just met Paul, attractive and forty, who worked in computers at Pacific Gas & Electric, I began to feel I was making right choices, and decided to leave my comfortable position as ad manager with a small travel magazine and attempt the world of sales. To my surprise I discovered I had a knack for it, and my sales began to soar along with Silicon Valley's surging economy.

This Mexico dream Paul and I were creating went back to my flower child roots and gave me hope that I still had a bohemian streak in my now borderline-bourgeois life.

Alejandro arrived mid-summer as planned and we had papers drawn up as fully as possible without actual parcel numbers and the legalese that accompanies land buys. We depleted our savings and wrote out a check to Alejandro and were one step closer to owning a beachfront lot on the Mexican Caribbean. To finance construction we planned to sell our California house but would wait until paperwork was finalized before taking that ultimate decisive action.

Every chance we had we ran back to Mexico. These trips were a quick fix for our serious addiction to the Mexican lifestyle. In December we went for Christmas, but before going to Puerto Morelos, we decided on a trip first to Merida, a colonial city and capital of the state of Yucatan. The pyramids at Chichen Itza were nearby, so we planned to use Merida as a base and do some exploring at the pyramids.

Merida filled pages in our guidebook. I loved having background about a place before arriving there, so I usually scoured bookstores before we left and bought everything in print about our destination. I discovered that Merida was the Yucatan's oldest city, dating back to 1542. In its heyday, during the henequen boom, it dealt with Spain, not Mexico City, for consul, thus setting Merida apart and giving it a distinctly European cultural identity. Merida gained fame and fortune from the green gold of henequen, a plant which produced a natural fiber used for making rope. By the early 1900s, henequen was used in Panama hats and during that time many Parisians moved to the Yucatan and became plantation owners. They transferred their new-found wealth into the construction of Victorian-style mansions along a street named *Paseo de Montejo*. Many still stand to this day.

We arrived December 23 and quickly located a hotel near the main plaza, Hotel Trinidad, in the tourist district. I spotted heavy wood and brass Spanish doors with "Open 24 Hours" painted at the top, and just had to see what was inside. On entering I discovered a hotel straight out of Barcelona, a tribute to bohemia everywhere. Bright mosaic tiles in wild patterns covered the floors and gaudy paintings with broken pieces of mirrors patterned into the frames decorated the walls. Comfortable, funky furniture looked inviting.

At the entrance behind an antique wooden bar that served as a reception area, a studious-looking desk clerk gazed up from a stack of papers and smiled. I looked beyond him to an unruly growth of areca palms and a cascade of other jungle style plants —ginger, heliconia, *flor de Maya*—all making up a bountiful interior garden.

"Do you have anything for tonight?" I asked, testing out my Spanish.

"*Seguro*," he responded. And within moments we checked into a room with sixteen-foot ceilings, no windows, and an enormous skylight that delivered all the light we needed. The hotel rooms faced the terrace courtyard and during the day many tourists left their doors open to take in fresh air and direct sunlight.

On Christmas Eve we awoke early and went to the bus station to catch a second class bus to Chichen Itza. Crowds thronged the depot that day, as many people were traveling for the holiday. In Mexico, as in Europe, December 24, *Noche Buena*, is celebrated as the feast of Christmas rather than Christmas Day. We were enroute to Piste, the small *pueblo* which served as a base for travelers coming and going to the popular ruins at Chichen Itza.

After a crowded bus trip, we were dropped off a few hours later on the highway near the pyramids. We grabbed our belongings and readied ourselves for the four kilometer walk, chatting excitedly to each other as we traipsed along. Overcast skies only intensified the heat and humidity. Even in a sleeveless dress I was not prepared for Yucatan temperatures. Paul managed the heat better than I did. We arrived at the entrance in good time, and were joined by other tourists on the way. One thing in our favor was the flat Yucatan ground—not a hill in sight—which made for easy walking.

As we rounded the last curve, we thought we would never see the splendor of Chichen Itza, and then we spotted the caretaker's hut and a stand of trees. By then we were accustomed to the climate and anxious to view the ruins. We paid the small fee, noticing the lack of pretension at one of the most well-known, best excavated sites in all the Maya world. This would change in later years, but in the mid '80s, Mexico's pyramid sites were lackadaisical at best in their security measures. Hearing about occasional thefts from the sites was never shocking.

In traveling more and more to the Yucatan, I'd begun to study the Maya culture and took every opportunity to see as many sites as could be squeezed into our vacation schedule. I'd already learned that Chichen Itza had more restored monuments to view than any other Maya archaeological site. It was the first Mayan ruin to be fully excavated, begun in 1923 by Sylvanus Morely of the Carnegie Institution in Washington. Morley, who was the prototype for Steven Spielberg's archeologist, Indiana Jones, excavated this site for nearly twenty years and what we saw bore witness to his labors. The immense structures had a scrubbed, white-washed appearance, with perfectly square hand-cut blocks stacked one on top of the other, using neither cement nor mortar. I stood there transfixed at the entrance, knowing now why I'd been struck with Maya-mania. How could I not be drawn into a study that boasted lost cities in the jungle, a secret hieroglyphic code, tombs of kings, buried treasure, and then the mysterious disappearance of this advanced civilization?

I'd read a theory that Chichen Itza's architecture was influenced by the Toltecs from Mexico's central valley. They overcame the Maya in a series of takeovers at the start of the post classic period (around 987 AD) and the Toltec's warring culture was attributed to the ritual and sacrifice that began to emerge in the Maya world. Early on, archaeological theory maintained the Maya were a non-violent people who had enjoyed a millennium of peace and had discovered the concept of zero. Perhaps before the Toltec invasion they were, but more recent views proved otherwise.

Speculation had it that at Chichen Itza the two cultures were fused together, which also incorporated the cult of the plumed serpent, *Quetzalcoatl* (*Kukulkan* in Maya) into the mix. Like D.H. Lawrence among others, I, too, was fascinated by this legend that invoked a tale of a Christ-like figure who departed and was expected to return generations later bringing salvation and redemption.

It was for *Quetzalcoatl* that the largest structure at Chichen Itza was built, Temple of *Kukulkan*, or *El Castillo*, as the Spanish later named it. On the edifice, protruding from each side of the limestone staircases, were serpents' heads.

At spring and fall equinox, the sun cast a remarkable shadow onto the temple, due to its placement in the heavens, the building's position, and the Maya's precise mathematical calculations prefigured centuries ago for this event. The shadow created the illusion of the serpent's body slithering down to the base of the staircase, finishing its journey at the serpent's mouth. A powerful image, it was witnessed twice a year by thousands of tourists who came to view this feat made possible by an ancient culture's ability to calculate the sun's effects on earth at equinox.

We saw groups of tourists like ourselves making their way up the 364 steps that led to the top plateau, which counted as the 365th step. (The Mayans configured the number of steps to coincide with the number of days in a year). Of course we climbed to the top, holding onto the safety chains that were placed there years ago for some traveling dignitary. After a slow ascent we stood at the apex, taking in the vast skyline and looking below at low, scrub jungle and the other pyramid structures scattered throughout the site. A handful of tourists reclined on the stairs or leaned against the rectangular limestone building. I watched a small Mayan boy fiddle with the wooden carving he was perfecting, oblivious to the crowds of people. On the far precipice a young Euro backpacker knelt beside his exhausted girlfriend, offering her a drink from his bottle of Evian.

We followed others inside the darkened stone chamber. Damp and cool, it harbored a cloistered staircase that led all the way to the bottom where the throne of the jaguar was located. I couldn't believe it was open to the public, especially in its decrepit condition. Only in Mexico. We squeezed down the slippery, narrow steps behind a parade of others and came out hundreds of feet below on the ground level half an hour later, gasping for air.

Later that night, after dark, we decided to take a chance and re-enter the park once everything was closed. We'd heard others had done it, and as security at the site barely existed, we stealthily made our way back to the pyramids and the Temple of *Kukulkan*, something that could never be done today. In the semi-darkness we inched our way to the top of the pyramid as the moon rose in the pre-Christmas sky.

For a brief moment, I felt as if I were thrust back in time. The moon's glow on the scrubbed limestone gave off an eerie shadow, and I have to admit I thought about the sacrifices that had taken place right where we sat, on the statue of *Chac Mool*. Did these sacrifices produce rain? Were they warriors or vestal virgins? And were their beating hearts really torn from their chests, as some accounts stated?

"What are you thinking?" Paul asked, as he inched nearer to

where I was sitting, sliding his arm around my back.

I snuggled against him and said, "Oh, nothing," deciding I'd share my thoughts on this at a later time. It was Christmas Eve, after all. Why ruin the moment? Better to wish on a star, I thought, as I gazed up at the brilliant night sky and wondered how on earth I got there.

———∗∗◦◦∗∗———

After the hustle-bustle of Merida, visiting the pyramids, and the long bus ride to Cancun, I was ready for the solitude of the coast and anxious to know what was happening with the land deal. When we got to Alejandro's a couple days later he gave us an update.

The deal was still moving slowly, he said. Sometimes with large properties it took the government longer to clear the title, he explained. We were patient because we still had to draw up plans for the house and then earn money to build it. It seemed a good time to talk house design. Alejandro sat down with us one afternoon and we brainstormed.

"When you build here in the Caribbean, look to the wind. Where do the trade winds come from?" he asked. "The trades come mostly from the south east, so we'll position the house to take advantage of these breezes. In the summer you'll be grateful for it."

He began to draw and came up with three basic boxes. "Your lot is large and quite long, so now you can move around these three boxes and see what works."

Paul began to get into the process, and having had experience as an architectural draftsman early on in his career, grasped the concept quickly. We cut out three boxes and started positioning them like rooms in a doll house. After a while, it became clear that we could overlap the boxes and stretch out the house. This design best utilized the land and also gave us plenty of square footage. So what we took with us that Christmas vacation was our house design, a very nice Christmas present indeed.

Paul had worked with Pacific Gas & Electric putting in a CAD system for computers. Since it was new and untried, the company encouraged employees to experiment on it. It was on this system that Paul designed plans for our house. In his off-hours he developed a computer generated blueprint, using the three boxes Alejandro had told us about. The final design we both agreed on was like a saw-tooth stretching ninety feet from bow to stern. Windows, lots of windows, were the focal point, and all rooms took full advantage of the ocean breeze.

That year, 1986, stretched on and Alejandro was now back in the States. He had finished construction on his house in Puerto Morelos and had built a small *bodega* on the property. Shaped like a pyramid, it was situated behind his house. He'd hired a Mayan named Jacinto to work as caretaker when he rented the house to tourists. We were surprised to hear business was brisk. Evidently, through placing ads in travel sections of large U.S. newspapers, he was managing to book his house on a regular basis. We were impressed . . . again.

And what was happening with the title on the property? we asked.

"That's why I'm back in the States," he told us. "There are many costs in preparing the infrastructure. We'll need electricity and roads. It will be expensive to clear the land. Also, I'm still looking for more investors so the project can continue to grow."

It was now summer 1986. Paul and I opted to not take a vacation until it was time to sign papers and set up our *fideicomiso*. Perhaps in November all would be set?

"There's a very good chance of it," said Alejandro. "Just keep your birth certificates ready. You'll need them when we have the *fideicomiso* drawn up."

That night I went home and dug out my birth certificate with my little baby feet inked permanently onto the parchment. What a weird thing to do to a baby, I thought.

"Paul, do you have a copy of your birth certificate?"

"We'll have to call my mom. If she doesn't have it we can get a copy at City Hall."

Paul is a native San Franciscan, third generation, something my midwestern heart often envied. His maternal Irish grandmother had lived through the 1906 earthquake. After the fires started in The City, as a child of six, she was shipped across the bay to Oakland with her name and destination pinned onto her coat. Nothing more. On his father's side, his strong-willed Italian grandmother had managed to run a successful restaurant and boarding house on Grant Avenue in North Beach while outliving three husbands and putting her son, Paul's father, through pharmacy college. Paul was firmly rooted in The City and proud of his California-Irish-Italian heritage, and no matter where he traveled, to him, San Francisco was home.

That week I went to City Hall and secured a copy of his birth certificate. Now we were both ready to be legal land owners in Mexico.

By October we had not heard from Alejandro and I was anxious to know what was happening with the land. Also, I hoped to take a Christmas vacation in Mexico if the title had cleared. Even though we avoided calling, not wanting to become a nuisance, I decided it had been long enough. I made the call and waited patiently while his secretary got him on the line.

"Hello, Jeanine. As a matter of fact, I had planned to call you. I have news about the land. Some important news," Alejandro said, dangling the sentence before me.

"Things have changed a bit, and I've been waiting for confirmation. Now I have it. It was looking a little bleak for a few months, and I didn't want to worry you and Paul, but here it is.

"It seems that the State of Quintana Roo has decided to pre-empt my purchase of the land near Playa del Carmen. The state needs that land to build a new car ferry to Cozumel. They are going to move it from Puerto Morelos to Playa del Carmen."

A thousand thoughts raced through my head. Pre-empted? Car ferry? "But Alejandro," I stammered. "What about our lot?"

"That's why I haven't called you for some time," he explained. "I've been in negotiations with the governor's office for several months now trying to sort this out. They're seizing it by eminent domain and they had planned on giving me fair market value for the property. Of course, their view of what the property is worth and my view differ widely. Since I purchased the property two and a half years ago, tourism has soared in Cancun and you've seen how Playa del Carmen has grown. They had only planned to give me $50,000 U.S. for the land, and I know it's worth much more than that."

By this time Paul was nearby and had sensed my anguish. He probably saw that I was hyperventilating.

"What's happening," he demanded. "What's going on?"

I lowered the phone's mouthpiece and spoke over it. "They've seized the land by eminent domain, and want to give Alejandro $50,000."

"What? Who seized it?" Paul yelled.

"But hold on, hold on," continued Alejandro. "I have more news. Better news. My brother has a friend in the governor's office, and he has convinced them that instead of simply giving me market value for the property, they should actually find another piece of land   beachfront land   and trade my land for this new property. It has taken a while to find something still available and a worthwhile swap. But we found land nearby. The parcel is much larger and it has potential, with a fresh water stream feeding into the ocean, and *cenotes.*"

Cenotes were freshwater pools or sink holes, common in the Yucatan, as the peninsula has only a few rare rivers above ground.

"Where is it?" I murmured, feeling I'd just been run over by a Mack truck.

"It's just four kilometers north of Playa. The land is close to *Capitán Lafitte.* Are you familiar with that property?"

Of course I was familiar with *Lafitte's.* It was a small, picturesque hotel with *palapas* on the beach and a restaurant. Quite the romantic setting, laidback, off the beaten track.

Well, that didn't sound so bad. *Lafitte's* beaches were something to behold, and maybe Alejandro had dodged the bullet by having friends in the governor's office. Maybe we would still own land in Mexico after all.

But this part of our adventure let us know one thing for certain . . . when buying land in a foreign country, fasten your seat belt, because anything can happen. We were heading for a very bumpy ride.

What's Going On?

Although we should have been prepared to expect the unexpected in a foreign land deal, the Mexico government's land seizure by eminent domain startled us. Along with the new venue and the unforeseen expansion came the need for more backing and the collateral to finance the make-over on this large, untamed piece of wilderness. Yes, it did have *cenotes*, three rivers, a rarity in the Yucatan, and jungles erupting with wild orchids and bromeliads, but it was also a demanding mistress requiring infinite cash. Funds were needed immediately so a road could be cleared to the beach. Without a road, no construction could begin.

The new land mass contained two hundred hectares. It was far more property than Alejandro had owned in Playa del Carmen, but the Playa land was more amenable. Access to power lines and water sources were already in place there. Creating a road at that location simply meant extending the existing road, but here on the new land, more effort was essential, and more manpower. To clear the property, heavy equipment was needed to carve a virgin roadway out of the thick, tangled jungle. This new infrastructure would require starting from scratch. There was nothing there. Nothing but mangroves and jungle. Just us and the wilderness.

So the shift began. Alejandro and his brother, Jorge, approached all landowners on both sides of the new site asking to buy their property. This, they explained, was a vital move. The land had much more potential than the old site due to its natural resources. With more room on either side, this wild beautification project could expand. We listened to their reasoning and had to agree. Alejandro compared the new property to what Epcot Center in Florida had been like, only decades earlier—mangroves, swamps, fresh water, and wildlife. Nothing landfill and vision couldn't change. This site had promise; now we just had to work with it.

We were in high spirits for our next trip to Mexico in March 1987. Alejandro had promised us a look at the new land, and it sounded like getting there would be a true-life adventure. We were to wear hiking boots and bring plenty of sunscreen and mosquito repellent; we were heading into the mangroves. We met Alejandro at his home in Puerto Morelos and he drove us to the work site at the new property. After driving south towards Playa del Carmen for twenty minutes we rounded an uncommon curve in the flat Yucatan landscape, and he pointed out a barely visible clearing alongside the jungle road, which he pulled into. A newly constructed *palapa* stood on the right side of the dirt driveway, where a few banana trees, leaves ruffled from the wind, grew in a cluster near the doorway. An old Mayan ventured towards us as the car pulled to a stop in front of him.

"Miguel!" exclaimed Alejandro as he opened the door and got out of the car. Miguel shuffled forward, shook Alejandro's hand, and then nodded shyly at us.

"Miguel sells cocos from the property to tourists and he's caretaker of the land."

That seemed to serve as a polite introduction, because then Alejandro said, "Come, we'll walk to the campsite." Already he was in hiking mode, and we promptly picked up our cadence and followed behind—first me, then Paul.

The thicket had recently been cut around the *palapa*, but

stopped sharply at a row of thick, tangled trees no more than one hundred feet ahead of us. Walking briskly to keep up with Alejandro, I noticed the rough terrain of the rugged road. It had been cut like a sheath through virtual scrub jungle and was barely wide enough to be called a path. As we walked, Alejandro pointed out numerous plants and flowers, including wild orchids, which curled into the trunks of trees. Mexico had hundreds of species of orchids, many found only in the Yucatan, he explained.

"Did you know orchids were one of the first flowering plants to evolve 120 million years ago? Very adaptable."

Just then a wisp of vine brushed across my face. "Watch the philodendrons," Alejandro said as he pushed vines out of the way in front of me, holding them back for a brief moment while I passed. Paul grabbed the vines from the other end, assuring me clear passage.

"The most common myth about orchids is that they're parasites," he continued, "but that's not correct. Orchids grow on trees, true, but they don't feed from them. They use the host merely as a place to be."

One of the things Paul and I both loved about Alejandro was his command of the land—in every explicable way. He could delve into dialogues on history, topography, plants and animals, environment, weather. His receptors were constantly being nudged by the wealth of information surrounding him in this jungle habitat, and then he put his spin on it. The man was, at heart, an environmentalist; however in Mexico, those rules would be stretched a bit. As a child of the '60s I respected this in him. I was all for saving the planet, or what was left of it. And Paul's prevailing pastime was gardening, as taught to him by his Irish grandfather in a tiny backyard plot in San Francisco. Paul had been no more than seven at the time, and growing things had become his talent; whatever he touched, grew. So both of us thoroughly enjoyed this nature hike with an environmentalist at the reins, doling out tidbits of information about the botanical resources of the area.

On approaching the camp we noticed a large rectangular *palapa* with a camp fire nearby. Stirring an oversized pot propped over an open fire was a dark-haired Mexican woman, trim and in her forties, who looked as if she would have been more at home behind a desk in an insurance firm than in this rustic jungle setting. She was introduced as Alejandro's sister-in-law, Rosa, Jorge's wife. In typical Maya fashion, she was cooking a stew that would feed the four men who were working the land alongside her husband. Whatever thoughts she may have had about the primitive situation she was in, she kept to herself. She spoke English with barely an accent, had lived in Texas for a while, and now, like both Alejandro and Jorge, had immersed herself in this massive land project.

The camp was tidy and well-kept and the *palapa,* made from the fronds of the utilitarian *chit* tree, served as housing for the four Mayan workers. Cotton hammocks hung in the corners; bunches of bananas in various stages of ripeness swung from rafters out of the way of jungle predators. I watched a scrawny feral cat stalk an oblivious gecko while Rosa went about her preparation for the mid-day meal. Paul chatted with Alejandro while Jorge stoked the fire.

Even on just arriving, we could see this new property had promise, but the task of clearing it and taming it seemed an overwhelming burden for only four men. After introductions and small talk, we continued on our way to the beach. At one point, the clearing had been unsuccessful, so we had to ford a small tributary at one of the rivers, searching out river rocks as stepping stones. Alejandro re-emphasized the land's diversity with these rivers, so rare in the Yucatan.

As we walked, he told us how he and Karla's cousin had first cut this swath of a path just months before. So thick was the jungle at the time that he could barely lift his machete above shoulder height to swing it. Although the encroachment bore testament to his work, it was still difficult to move forward at an even pace. Thank God we'd remembered the mosquito repellent. The sunscreen seemed less of a necessity, but the combination of water and heat created a perfect breeding ground for one of the world's most annoying insects.

Following Alejandro into the jungle seemed like our very own adventure land, better than any E-ticket ride I'd ever taken at Disneyland. What could be better? I thought, as I sloshed my way through ankle-deep sludge, soaking my new Zodiac hiking boots in the foulest water they would ever encounter.

Once past the river, we could hear the rushing sound of fresh water meeting the ocean downstream. It seemed to beckon and we all picked up the pace. After walking another five minutes, at last we saw the ocean and the long windswept beach. To us bedraggled city folks, it was the complete picture of paradise. Delicate palm trees stretched high into a never-ending sky where one or two cumulus clouds hung in perfect stillness. It looked more like a backdrop for a south seas musical than anything remotely real. Paul and I stood in awe. I was barely breathing as I took in the landscape and the vista—wide beach, whitest sand imaginable. The heat and humidity of the jungle path had vanished, as had the mosquitoes. We breathed ocean smells.

"Here you have it!" Alejandro announced with a smile that showed his pride at the beauty he had helped uncover. "This is the center of the property where the three rivers meet. I plan to build my house here. It will overlook the *cenote* over there. What do you think?"

Words failed me.

Just beyond the rushing river lay the *cenote*. A *cenote*, Alejandro explained, raising his voice just enough so we could hear him over the river sounds, was a fresh water pool of incredibly clear, cold water. Since the Yucatan had few rivers above ground, these became the water source for the Mayans, wells that had been formed by the crumbling of the limestone crust just above the underground rivers. Would we like to see the *cenote*?

We all forded the river again, drenching our shorts as we held our boots now overhead. It wasn't easy playing Tarzan and Jane for the day, I was beginning to realize. And it was no small feat getting to the *cenote*.

Encroaching green foliage surrounded the fifty foot wide pool of water, displaying a backdrop of primeval forest. No other water I'd ever seen compared with its clarity. At first glance I thought I saw reflections of trees above the water level. Only after closer observation did I realize I was seeing mangrove tree trunks that stretched up from the bottom of the *cenote* to thirty or forty feet above the water line. The water was as clear as a green diamond, I could see to its very depths.

The Yucatan never failed to surprise and excite me, for although I was no stranger to nature, the things I saw there were indescribably different from the Mother Nature to which I'd grown accustomed. The river noise made it difficult to talk, although all three of us were so mesmerized by the beauty of the surrounding scene, little needed to be said. After ten minutes or so, Alejandro motioned with his hand towards the river, and with that gesture we headed back towards the path that had led us to the ocean.

Once back on the beach, he said, "Your lot will be the last one on the property down at the southern end. This will give you more privacy, too, as you will be bordered by empty land on one side. Would you like to walk to the property line and see it?"

We answered simultaneously, yes. That was what we came here for, wasn't it? To see the land, to compare it to the original property we had once almost owned. Waves lapped rhythmically against the shore, and I waded through them, testing the temperature of the Caribbean water as we followed Alejandro down the beach to the property line.

I'm happy to say we were not disappointed with the end lot. And because it had depth, we walked back into the encroaching jungle to claim what someday would be ours.

"You can begin your footprint at this palm tree," motioned Alejandro, as he stepped off footage, "and take the house back to here."

I looked to where he was pointing; he had drawn a line in the soft black dirt. I walked over to where he stood, and observed, from his vantage point, what the house placement would be like.

"The lot is so long, you can always build a smaller cottage in the back," he continued.

"Some day you may want to build a *bodega* like I've done for Jacinto."

Building a small cottage for a caretaker sounded like a good plan to us. We were aware of Alejandro's success in renting his beach house in Puerto Morelos as a tourist rental. We thought we might copycat the idea he had implemented to help pick up some costs we would spend on construction.

We didn't know exactly when we could escape city life, certainly not in the immediate future. We still needed a master plan and renting out our little piece of paradise to others until we could use it full time sounded ideal.

In watching Alejandro actualize his plans we were learning fast. He and Karla had spent large sums on advertising to entice travelers to their section of the Riviera Maya. Through their trial and error we would know how to advertise our own beach house some day. We were eager students and thankful to have attentive mentors with money on their minds. For money was what it would take to pull this off. Money and luck.

You Can't Always Get What You Want

Ever since meeting Alejandro on that remote Cobá road while waiting for a bus, we lived and breathed Mexico. The project was never far from our thoughts and we talked about it constantly to bolster our spirits as time moved along and we had nothing to show for it. We'd told countless friends and relatives about our Mexico plans, of course, and eventually the questions began to surface about our mysterious land deal in Mexico. We were in a holding pattern, and all of a sudden everyone we knew wanted to know why the delay. When we explained the nuances of buying land in a foreign country, we began to see their looks of reproach.

"You bought that land a couple years ago, so where's your title?" one of our closest friends asked point blank after seeing a *Sixty Minutes* segment on buyers bilked out of land in foreign countries. "Are you sure it's safe to buy land in Mexico?"

We assured him all was well, and although unexpected problems had cropped up, this would make it all the sweeter once things were settled. The fact was, we believed in Alejandro and the new land project. After we hiked the jungle property with him and saw how massive it was, we realized there was more at stake with this land. We also felt the new deal offered him an opportunity to regroup after his first plan fell through, thanks to the Mexican government's strong-arming.

To us, the new location was even more advantageous as it offered more privacy than the Playa del Carmen land. We had to admit, it was another ideal situation, but now, our friend was right, it was time to set things in motion.

Although we pretended calm, we were both feeling nervous about how long Alejandro had been absorbed in the project and the lack of any apparent progress.

The house plans, by this time, were complete. Alejandro had looked them over and given his approval; we were putting money aside for starting costs, and when we were sure the title was transferred and the *fideicomiso* was in our names, we were prepared to make the ultimate commitment and sell our California house to finance the Mexico construction. Since we knew it would still take years to escape the 9 to 5 world, after our house sold we'd rent in the Bay Area until the time came to leave the city. Our plans were linear: Mexico—home—retirement.

It was July 1988 and I called Alejandro at his San Francisco office to arrange a meeting to discuss the land deal and see if the *fideicomiso* title had cleared. If it had, we planned to take a trip south combining business and pleasure. I hoped for a useful working vacation to get things set up in Mexico so we could begin building. I was anxious for time off from my work as a sales rep. My stress level was at the red alert stage. I was chained to desk and clients. I needed a break.

Karla met us at the door and we entered Alejandro's new city offices. They were yuppie-trendy with a predominance of re-worked wood. Very spiffy. Apparently the office had been an old market at one time; large bay windows faced the street bringing in late afternoon sun. It was summer in the City, and Potrero Hill, where his offices were located, was the banana belt, warm and sunny. Directly in front of the window sat an old Mercedes, beautifully restored. It was a sleek, four-door sedan, long and black. Alejandro's new car. Things were looking up, no more rusted-out Honda. He was gaining prestige and business, apparently, was brisk.

We sat down and waited for a lull. All the appropriate magazines, Architectural Digest, Forbes, Fortune, were arranged on a stylish, mahogany coffee table in front of us. The man obviously led two lives, I thought, as I took in my surroundings. And he could work well in both worlds—Mexico outback or full bore city. A true chameleon.

A moment later Alejandro appeared from a back office and Karla motioned us towards a desk in the rear. After pleasantries were exchanged we got down to business. I jumped right in, saying, "I'd like to take a vacation soon and thought we could incorporate signing papers at the same time. Are we close to securing the title for the land?"

"Well," Alejandro said as he shifted positions in an expensive leather office chair that looked as if it came out of a Sharper Image ad, "it hasn't gone as smoothly as I'd planned. We had hoped by now that we'd have clear title to the land, but because we've been buying parcels on either side, things aren't finalized yet. I can't say when we'll be able to put papers in your name. It could still be a while. Maybe in the spring."

"Spring?" I asked, shocked. "You mean eight or nine months? It's July now."

"Yes, I don't foresee anything sooner, plus there are lots of things that need to be done on the road and infrastructure before we can even contemplate building houses."

"I don't think I can wait . . ." I murmured, feeling a catch in my throat. I hadn't planned on having a meltdown in Alejandro's designer office, but I naively believed we were close to signing papers for the land title. This setback, yet another, was unforeseen and definitely unplanned . . . at least in my book.

"It seems like we've been waiting a long time," I pleaded. "Can I ask what's holding things up?"

A steely look crossed Alejandro's face. "Well, I'm sorry you're upset, Jeanine," his voice raised an octave. "But you must understand it hasn't been easy for us either this past year. We've had to make a lot of concessions ourselves, and we're trying to get more investors involved, large-scale investors, so we can better promote the project. Because the land's ecology is so unique, with the *cenote* and the rivers, we believe we can create a park with a marina plus a restaurant and hotel along with condos and lots for sale. We're leaning towards a multi-layered enterprise . . . and that takes time."

I took a quick inventory of the upscale office, gazed out the window at his fancy, black Mercedes, listened to the incessant ringing of the phones with more clients, more business. Then it hit me. Alejandro had no reason to hurry. He had arrived. I began to feel Paul's and my place in his "multi-layered" enterprise fell near the bottom.

"Also," I heard him say, bringing me back to the moment, "we had some bad luck recently. In order to attract investors, the way business is done in Mexico is with a handshake and a smile. Nothing more. I thought I had the right person for the project, someone who was going to help us begin the infrastructure.

"Well, he was not honorable, not to be trusted. He's simply disappeared, and we have to start all over again. Everything has been pushed back because of my lack of judgment. So it's imperative that we find more investors," he ended lamely.

I pulled myself together as I heard these final words declaring disaster. Oh, no! I thought. *Another* setback. We've been trying to put this land deal together for three years, maybe longer. We're ready to put our house on the market; we have money in savings; our blueprints are ready for a contractor.

"I understand, Alejandro," I said, backpedaling as I began to get the big picture. "I've been under a lot of stress at work and I was really counting on a vacation in a few months. We know you're under pressure pulling this together. Maybe we'll go to Mexico just to get away, with no expectation on the land right now."

I realized it would do no good to buck the system and try to strong arm our project manager and benefactor. Even though I could throw a hissy fit with gusto, I had the distinct impression Alejandro would outdo me at it, hands down. No need to rush into an emotional scene just yet; there would be plenty of time for that.

⟶►●◄⟵

I stared out the car window as we drove down the coast to Half Moon Bay that evening, catching a rare glimpse of the Farallone Islands far out at sea. The summer sun was in its final phase of slipping into the ocean as my anger overtook me again. I was rapidly losing faith in our man south of the border and his glorified project.

"Where do we fit into this large-scale project?" I asked Paul. "Aren't we his oldest investors? Doesn't that count for anything?"

"I don't know," Paul responded, apparently just as puzzled as I was. "But it seems he needs to attract more high-end investors to pull this off. I don't think he's connected. He needs friends in high places—you know, the people who buy hotel chains and time share companies. Or why not try to find Japanese investors? They're buying beaches everywhere else, why not Mexico?"

I pulled my hair back, a nervous gesture, and said, "Maybe he simply can't afford this project. He probably could have worked it out at the other site, but now with this massive scale, doesn't he need big money?"

"I'd say so," Paul agreed. "The infrastructure alone will run at least a million, even in Mexico. You've seen the dimensions of the land. From the highway to the beach it's easily three kilometers. He needs a good road, electricity, water hookups, and let's face it—he's working with a staff of four Mayans. I think development is still a long way off."

It was obvious to both of us that we were at a crossroads with Alejandro. Our choices—either chill out, or wait patiently until he had things ready to go. Mexico was becoming our unattainable Holy Grail, and the pursuit of it had taken on epic proportions. Little did we realize what lay ahead was something neither of us could have fathomed, and far beyond anyone's control.

El Huracán

Just when it seemed things could get no worse with our latent "Mexican time" land deal, Mother Nature stepped in to remind us how insignificant our plans were, and how much further out of control the situation could go. Enter Hurricane *Gilberto*, September 14, 1988, a class-five storm named hurricane of the century. Now what?

I called Alejandro at his office and Karla answered.

"What's happened to your beach house in Puerto Morelos?" I asked.

"We don't know yet," Karla paused, then continued. "I'm on pins and needles waiting to hear something, but all the electricity and phone lines are out. We're hoping the sea wall has protected the house."

A picture of their sea wall flashed into my mind. More an afterthought, it was no more than three rocks in height, one stacked on top of the other, Mayan style. Very little, if any, cement had been used and to me, it looked more decorative than functional.

Well, one can always hope, I thought to myself. There's always divine intervention. Maybe Guadalupe, patron saint of Mexico, worker of miracles, had stepped in and saved his house from the deluge.

It would be a tense few days before any news was out regarding the hurricane's damage, and when it came, it was horrific. Hurricane *Gilberto* had been classified as a five, topping the

National Weather Service's Saffir-Simpson rating scale, with winds over two hundred miles an hour.

When news did come, the reports were devastating. Cancun was flattened and tourists had been herded into city hotels for protection. The airport was still closed. No one had water and the food supply was dwindling as all major roads in the state were out of commission, so no supplies could get through. Cancun was one large disaster area, inaccessible by air and land. It was impossible to get fresh information from the region.

A few days later we heard from Karla. "Bad news," she began. "Alejandro's house is gone, totally destroyed. It blew away . . . into the sea, into the jungle. Who knows where? It's gone and now we have to return rental money we were holding for tourists who'd reserved the house for high season. I don't know when we'll be able to repay them. We used the money for the new project."

Nothing like a setback to a setback. I was speechless. My mouth couldn't even begin to form words to respond. And my mind? My mind was scrambled. Paul and I watched The Weather Channel constantly, hoping to catch news about the hurricane damage.

As more information filtered out, we heard Puerto Morelos, the charming fishing village where Alejandro had built his stylish beach house, had been Point Zero. Rumor had it that nothing was left standing on the beach; it was ravaged and looked like an atomic bomb had been detonated. News reports finally confirmed Cancun's sparkling new hotel zone was demolished and it would take years to rebuild what had been destroyed.

I thought of the cynical joke my friend often repeated when things went amiss—"How do you make God laugh?" Answer—"Tell him your plans." Ours certainly needed adjusting.

We were clearly in shock. But we knew our concerns were

nothing compared to what Alejandro was going through. This could certainly be *sayonara* for his Mexico project.

In a month, we called Alejandro's office and ever-present Karla answered.

"Things are difficult," Karla told me. "We're busy returning rental money on the beach house."

"What a process, Karla," I sympathized. "How's Alejandro?"

"Oh, he's doing okay. He plans to go to Mexico next month and see how bad it is. Jorge told us the winds were so strong that the palm trees look as if they were burned in a forest fire. Wind damage, with that force, will create such a burn."

I hadn't thought about the trees, or now, the lack of them. Depression set in all over again when I realized those tall, delicate coco palms on the beach had been destroyed. To me, they were as much a part of the beach as the sand and the water.

Hurricanes commonly ravaged the Caribbean every fall. In looking back at storm tracks throughout the region, as early as 1515, major hurricanes had been recorded passing over the islands of Puerto Rico, the Virgin Islands and the Dominican Republic, but since Cancun was such a new city, incorporated in the late '70s shortly after Quintana Roo had been made the 31st state of the Mexican Union, there was no research to substantiate how often the region had been the target of a major storm. Oddly enough, I'd never even thought about a possible hurricane hitting Cancun, much less Puerto Morelos.

"What happened to Puerto Morelos?" I was curious to know.

"Most everything on the beach is gone. There are no homes left standing on the ocean. A few houses across the road may have survived, but for the most part, it's totally destroyed."

I thought back to the last time we'd been in Puerto Morelos. I remembered sitting in a *palapa* restaurant, watching two Mayan boys working on remodeling a building across the street, and finally white-washing it. Other businesses were also going through renovation. Two new restaurants had sprung up, and bilingual menus were appearing at a few local eateries, a sure sign that change was expected. The town was poised and ready for discovery, a deb at her cotillion, anticipating her turn on the staircase.

For a moment, the memory of Mexico overwhelmed me. I took a deep breath, a sigh, really and felt incredible sadness. I felt sorry for Alejandro, for Puerto Morelos. I felt sorry for everyone.

Then it hit me. What about our plans? We had waited, too. But until I actually heard the news firsthand from Karla, I hadn't believed it could be this much of a disaster. I'd been in denial, hoping some luck would come into play.

"It sounds like a desperate situation," I told Karla. "Please tell Alejandro how deeply sorry we are to hear this. I'll call again in a month and see how things are going."

In January we saw Alejandro at his San Francisco office and heard a first hand account of *Gilberto's* wrath.

"Cancun is in a tailspin. They've lost the entire season, although a few of the larger hotels in the hotel zone have made enough repairs to get through this year. Many are offering discounts to lure tourists," Alejandro told us, rubbing his forehead. I noticed his hair was beginning to gray around the temples and knew this catastrophe had taken its toll on him.

"But you have to imagine what the city looks like. There's rubble everywhere—huge blocks of concrete and pieces of rebar lying in the streets, houses torn in half. The foliage is gone. All trees and plants were destroyed by the wind, and there's no wildlife because the windburn destroyed their food sources.

"Near Puerto Juarez and Punta Sam, the two small ports for Isla Mujeres, large boats, approaching ship size, were pushed out of the water and onto the land by the surge and haven't been removed. You can't imagine the amount of damage."

"And Puerto Morelos?" I asked, eager for any news from the front.

"Puerto Morelos is another story. As you know, it was really coming along, hoping to attract more tourists this year. Well, everything on the beach is gone or badly damaged. The only hotel south of Cancun with any luck at all was Hotel *Lafitte* near Playa and the land. They had insurance and hired hundreds of workers to rebuild the *cabañas* and restaurant. They're hoping to re-open for Christmas. Almost every other business south of Cancun is in turmoil or on hold."

We were shell-shocked but we weren't clueless. I knew this meant another indefinite delay. How much bad luck could befall this one guy, I mused silently. He was neck and neck with the original Job as far as I could tell. Of course the subject had to be broached about, well, the unspeakable. The land, our sadly maligned project. Since I'd already established myself as a sparing partner, I figured I'd step into the ring again. I was several years into my job as a sales rep, and dealing with corporate fallout had given me a thick skin.

I braced myself and ventured, "I hope this doesn't sound unreasonable to ask at this time, but do you have any idea how this will affect the land project?" I tried to let the words slip out as gently as possible before the emotional explosion took place.

"Jeanine, you can't expect me to worry about the land *now* when I have renters to re-pay since my house was destroyed by a hurricane," Alejandro snarled, his voice rising with, I assumed, his blood pressure. He gave me a withering look.

Bingo. I felt I had just been awakened from a dream. No, a nightmare. I was in a dimly lit elevator, descending all the way down to the bottom floor, basement level, of some unknown place. I imagined I heard a subdued bell announce the floor's arrival; the doors opened with a soft swoosh, and before me, there were flames everywhere—an inferno.

As only dreams can do in their own inherent way, I somehow knew I could not stay in that elevator. But then again, how could I leave it and step into the fiery blaze? My mind searched madly for an escape. It came to me in an instant. To free myself from this situation, I had to fly . . . fly above those flames to safety.

And that is precisely what I did. I was on a Mexicana flight to Cancun one month later.

———⇒⊷⊷⊷⊷———

Within forty-eight hours after our arrival in Quintana Roo, we'd found a new contractor. He showed us a beachfront lot, we fell in love with it, and he set us up with an attorney in Merida who would prepare our *fideicomiso*. From the flames into the fire, I told myself as we drove the back roads to Merida, through Mayan villages with *palapa* huts and *topes*, the formidable road bumps designed to force cars to reduce speed; past clusters of wide-eyed children peddling orange slices in plastic cups, and bags-of-bones mutts, sprawled carelessly along the dusty roadside.

We were engaging in Plan B. After our last episode with Alejandro I'd had an epiphany. Alejandro needed new blood to make his project gel, and without it, this setback could last indefinitely. Maybe forever.

It finally hit me. If we waited for Alejandro to get organized, we might never build a house in Mexico. Perhaps in time he would resolve his problems, but did we have time to wait? My primary fear was if Alejandro failed to pull together his end of the bargain, in twenty years when Paul and I looked back on our lives, would we say we *almost* built a house in Mexico, but because of our contractor, our dream went unfulfilled? I didn't want our aspirations to be thwarted by someone else's lost opportunity.

Once we became objective about the situation, we began to look at Alejandro's land deal as a long term investment, something we could hold onto for the future. But for the present, we needed land we could start building on tomorrow.

We flew into Cancun with no hotel reservations and rented a car at the airport, then drove to Puerto Morelos and looked for a place to stay. Even though it was high season, tourists were noticeably absent from the landscape, thanks to the recent hurricane. Even without tourists, however, there were few hotels from which to choose. *Cabañas La Ceiba*, the ten-room hotel near where Alejandro's house had stood, and another set of *cabañas, Ojo de Agua*, had disappeared in the storm.

Both had been beachfront; neither had constructed sea walls to curb the storm surge. These hotels might have hoped the Palancar Reef would protect Puerto Morelos, acting as a natural sea wall. But when waves are high, they can top the reef and submerge it, giving the shoreline a beating and obliterating homes, hotels, whatever is in the path, as with *Gilberto*.

Storm tides on the other hand can be caused from the cumulative effect of strong winds pushing water in the same direction for a long time. If the wind pushed towards land, the water had to pile up when it hit the coastal incline along the shore, causing a virtual wall of water. Whatever had claimed *Cabañas La Ceiba* and *Ojo de Agua*—wave action or storm tides—wasn't really important. Both were gone now.

In town, charming *Posada Amor* was booked with Europeans taking advantage of rock bottom hurricane discounts all up and down the Tulum Corridor, as the coast was then called. The Riviera Maya moniker wouldn't come until years later. *Posada* was listed in all the guide books as a reasonable place to stay for backpackers on a budget. It was an old reliable stand-by and almost always full.

The only other choice in town was Hotel Paradise, the very antithesis of its name, and situated at the edge of the mangroves. It had eighteen rooms, ten upstairs, eight down, and in spite of its cell block austerity, it was clean. We requested a room upstairs hoping for a stray ocean breeze in the late afternoon.

After talking a few moments with the friendly desk clerk, we decided to take one night until we figured out what we were doing. Did we want one *cama* or two? she asked.

Neither of us knew the translation of *cama*. Finally after a lot of discussion, we understood the meaning—bed.

One would be fine, we told her. Then we lugged our baggage upstairs to our Puerto Morelos suite. On entering I wondered who had stolen the furniture. The room was empty except for a double bed and ceiling fan. The walls, bearing nothing but a coat of bright, blue paint, were accented by turquoise floor tile. While at Hotel Paradise, we would experience an ant attack, a power surge through my electric curlers that burned a hole in the acrylic bedspread, and malodorous swamp smells, but all this came for $12 U.S. a night. When we stayed in these Mexican-style hotels, we never doubted where we were. This was part of our south-of-the-border adventure—no white bread Holiday Inn for us. What we liked about Quintana Roo was you couldn't find anything *chic* south of the Cancun hotel zone in those pre-all-inclusive days on the coast.

We unpacked our belongings and after a quick, cold shower decided to walk into *el centro* in search of dinner. Strolling along the beach, we noticed most existing structures were badly damaged. The Amar Inn, a rustic bed and breakfast with *palapas*, had been torn in half. All that was left of the sign painted on the roof top was the forlorn *"amar."* Love.

The beach seemed much wider than before the storm. Apparently, *Gilberto's* raging tides had deposited more sand, extending it fifty feet farther out. This was the storm's only benefit, a backhanded payment for the tragedy it had imposed.

We heard that after the storm, squatters came from all over the Yucatan to homestead this new beachfront property. In Mexico, if someone occupies certain public lands for an extended period of time, squatters' rights prevail and the land is legally theirs. Just days before the new beach land qualified for this legal loophole, depositing titles into the hands of indigenous Mayans, the PRI's federal army arrived in Puerto Morelos and relocated the squatters.

Behind the Pemex Gas Station on the main highway, jungle was cleared, and the squatters were given land grants. Within weeks, stick houses sprang up, made from the common *chaca* and *chit* trees, with dirt floors, no running water, no toilets, no electricity. This area, more shanty town than *pueblo,* came to be known as *el Crucero,* the crossroads.

Although this type of living was the standard for sixty percent of the world population, it was a surprise to see it so close to Puerto Morelos.

Today most of the shanty town is gone, but many of the shacks still have neither running water nor bathrooms. Occasionally a zealous mayor will initiate upgrades, but higher living standards are still a long way off for *el Crucero,* now known as the *"Colonia."* So much yet to learn about my soon-to-be-adopted country.

Our after-the-hurricane walking tour continued to the square. The town lacked life. Even the small grocery store on the corner was closed. No restaurants were open. We were forced to walk back to the hotel, get in the car and drive further south to find a place to eat. Along the highway, we found a rustic little restaurant. It appeared to be the only place open for miles.

We walked in and surveyed the darkened, nearly empty eatery. In one corner, a coatimundi, resembling a cross between a raccoon and a cuddly monkey, with a pointed white snout and long, flat tail, was tied with a rope. The only diners, a middle-aged Mexican couple, sat in the back of the room. Another couple stood near the kitchen; apparently they owned the restaurant and the man checked us out as he walked over with menus.

He was a bit disheveled, had a swarthy look, needed a shave, and spoke English. I pegged him as an expatriate with an attitude. He had a touch of Jimmy Buffet, but just barely; he lacked the spit and polish.

"Did you want to eat?" the question rhetorical as he tossed a couple of worn-out menus our way.

We nodded glumly and started reading. The offerings were basic but sounded tasty enough. Even though the atmosphere was rough it was the only thing open for miles. The menu man returned to the back of the restaurant and started to argue quietly with the pretty Mexican woman who had taken a seat at a table, probably his wife, I surmised.

With few choices on the menu, we quickly decided on dinner. Also, the corner conversation in the back was picking up steam and we thought we'd better order before the kitchen closed for the night. Then the coatimundi began chattering, obviously wanting to get into the act. Oh, boy. A marital meltdown plus a chattering monkey in a dimly lit *palapa* restaurant. Maybe this *was* Margaritaville; all we needed to complete the scene was an eight-track tape of Buffett for background effect. Finally the conversation in the back ended and the man wandered over to our table.

"Have you decided?" he asked, not much for small talk. "Oh,

did I mention we're out of everything but the enchiladas. I got two servings left. Do you want 'em?"

"Guess we'll take the enchiladas," Paul said wryly. "And a couple of *cervezas*? *Dos Equis*?"

"Yea, I'll bring them," the man responded over his back shoulder, walking away. A few moments later two not-so-cold beers arrived, but we were thirsty and tired and just the fact they were liquid had a calming effect.

Things quieted down at the back table, the other couple left, the coatimundi dozed off, and we tried not to notice the general overall grubbiness of the place. In fifteen minutes our dinners arrived. The entrees looked edible, but I noticed I was missing silverware.

"Excuse me," Paul called to the owner, "could we please get another fork and knife?"

"Okay," he responded as he started back towards the kitchen, pausing at the table that had just been vacated moments before by the other diners. Thinking I couldn't see him, he grabbed a fork and wiped it on his shirt, then turned around and headed our way.

"Here's your fork," he said, slinging it on the table and darting off before I could protest.

"Oh, God!" I moaned in complete disbelief.

"What's the matter?" Paul asked.

"Did you see that? I am *not* using that fork! How gross. Can I borrow your spoon?"

"What did he do?"

"Remember the couple sitting at the back table? He just grabbed a fork from their table and wiped it on his shirt! God, I know this is Mexico, but it's not Tijuana! *Bienvenidos.* Welcome to Mexico, my eye!"

Within minutes both owners had mysteriously disappeared

into the kitchen, their voices rising another octave, no doubt a continuation of their connubial bliss. I heard pots banging, then a crash as one skidded into the sink. Well, at least I knew the argument wasn't over washing dishes. I borrowed Paul's spoon and knife and scooped up my food that night. If I rated my Mexican dining experiences, this would rank as one of the most unpleasant. All it needed to bottom out would be coming down with Moctezuma's revenge in the morning.

We deposited pesos with the bill our Jimmy Buffet wanna-be had dropped on the table with the entrees, left no tip, and split. Once in the car, heading back to Hotel Paradise, I realized how tired I was, but also how excited I felt being back in Mexico on a new adventure . . . in spite of that strange little restaurant.

Aftermath

When looking up Puerto Morelos in my travel guide, a scant two sentences summarized it, making mention only of *Posada Amor*, the car ferry to Cozumel, and the army outpost. It was, indeed, Quintana Roo's best kept secret. The archaic little town, now mostly rubble, had been passed over for the newly renovated Playa del Carmen with its fabulous, wide beaches. Puerto Morelos couldn't compete in that department; its beaches emitted a natural beauty, more Frida Kahlo to Playa's Carmen Miranda.

But waking up in Puerto Morelos gave me the feeling of opportunity knocking. I felt I was on the verge of a breakthrough with our land project. We arose early the next morning anxious to test our luck and to tell the desk clerk we'd decided to stay at Hotel Paradise for another few nights. The woman behind the desk looked so familiar, and after a short conversation I realized we knew her from another Puerto Morelos hotel we stayed at years before.

When we disclosed our plans on purchasing land, she said her husband was a realtor and contractor, and she suggested there were several lots for sale on the beach right in Puerto Morelos.

We arranged to meet her husband, Rodolfo, that morning. She gave us directions to her house and we arrived there minutes later. Her house sat on the beach, a truncated structure, more fort-like than villa-esque. We knocked on the imposing Spanish-style door and a corpulent man with a bushy, black mustache, opened it. He was wearing a light blue *guayabera* shirt and dress slacks, and looked the part of a typical Mexican businessman.

A filtered cigarette emitted a steady stream of smoke from his right hand, and then he said, "Can I help you?" his voice a bit wary, as if mentally weighing us.

Thank goodness he speaks English, I thought to myself.

"Your wife sent us, from the hotel, "Paul started. "She said you're a realtor."

"Come in, come in," his arm extended as he ushered us into a massive foyer leading to an atrium with high ceilings which opened onto an inner courtyard. An interior swimming pool, sporting a light patina of green sludge, occupied center stage. Typically Mexican in décor, the room radiated airiness and warmth, and in spite of the pool growth, it was impressive. His office was the first room off the entryway to the right, and he showed us two leather chairs. We were seated and Paul spoke first.

"We've been coming to this area for years," Paul began as he settled into his seat. "Now we're looking for beachfront land. We've stayed all up and down the coast. In fact, we used to stay at your *cabañas*. I'm sorry to hear they were so badly damaged in the hurricane."

"Yes, the hurricane. . ." Rodolfo's voice trailed off. "The hurricane ruined so many things on the beach, including the hotel and *cabañas*. Such a terrible storm. It will take years to recover from *Gilberto*, both for Puerto Morelos and Cancun."

"We noticed a lot of damage to the town," Paul continued. "Was Puerto Morelos hit harder than Cancun?"

Rodolfo stroked his mustache and said, "They say Puerto Morelos was point zero, but maybe Playa del Carmen was hit worst. No one really knows for sure. I've also heard point zero may have been Hotel *Capitán Lafitte*. Do you know it?" he asked as we nodded our heads in recognition.

"*Lafitte*, too, was destroyed, but they had insurance and are rebuilding. There are hundreds of workers there now . . . they plan to re-open this week for high season," Rodolfo continued.

Everything in and around Cancun, we were soon to find out, revolved around "high season," which began at Christmas and lasted through the end of April, just past Easter and *Semana Santa*, the equivalent of our Holy Week in the States. When the U.S. was in a dead winter slump it was simply heaven on the Caribbean coast. Average temperatures ranged in the low eighties and there was always a light breeze off the ocean. By May, Caribbean temperatures began to rise along with the humidity, and tourists thinned out. No business. During the dog days of summer, Puerto Morelos became *Muerto* Morelos. Dead. This meant businesses needed to make their money in a few short months, and basically starve the rest of the year.

"Did many people have insurance?" Paul asked.

"Not many," Rodolfo answered. "It is a pity."

"I'm sorry to hear it. How did your house withstand the storm, being right on the beach?"

"We were very, very lucky," said Rodolfo, crossing himself like a Catholic priest dispensing penance. Then he continued, "We built a sea wall plus a large terrace. Would you like to see it?"

This certainly piqued our interest. Here was a house that withstood the storm. We were anxious to see what Rodolfo had done to spare his house from *Gilberto's* devastation.

We followed him around the swimming pool to the rear of the courtyard, beyond the spacious, tiled kitchen to the French doors in back. Two jet black toucans, intent on eating a ripe mango, looked down on us from their perch in a splendid gilded cage. An unassuming maid, sweeping with swift, syncopated strokes, pushed her well-worn broom to the side as we walked by. She gave us a shy, curious smile as we stepped around the pile of dust she had accumulated.

As Rodolfo opened the French doors, we looked out onto an extensive concrete patio, unpainted, thirty feet wide and stretching towards the beach. Although it wouldn't win any awards for beauty, apparently it was worth every peso he paid for it.

"This," said Rodolfo as he pointed at the concrete terrace, "this is what saved my house. It was the terrace, the concrete below, then the sea wall that kept us safe."

We walked over to the sea wall and noticed it was twelve feet higher than ground level and solid, probably two feet wide. Quite a wall. So this combination saved his house from the destruction we had seen everywhere else.

"No one thought about hurricanes when they were building, because Cancun is a young city, only twelve years old. Hurricanes don't happen every year, and since no one lived on this coast until recently, no one bothered to think about storms. Until the last several years, Quintana Roo was home only to the *chicleros*, the Chan Santa Cruz Indians, and long before that, to the pirates. Have you heard the stories?"

Fast becoming a buff on local Quintana Roo history, I'd learned the *chiclero* tree tappers had been hired by Wrigley in the early 1900s to tap the *chicle*, or *sapodilla*, trees for the sap made famous by chewing gum. When a synthetic ingredient was later discovered in 1935, chickle prices fell, business decreased, and the population of Quintana Roo declined. Then in the late 1950s the federal government deeded land to these *chicleros* in an attempt to try and tame the territory of Quintana Roo, and give some competition to the Chan Santa Cruz Indians who had been its only inhabitants since the Caste War of 1847.

Each *chiclero* received fifty hectares of land, one hundred and twenty five acres. Some said the *chicleros* were as cut throat as the Chan Santa Cruz. But to live the life they led, often alone, deep in the tropical forests where many faced death from snakes, wild animals, or marauding Indians, they had to be toughened, crusty men.

Before that, pirates had inhabited the coast on and off since the 17th century, when booty was plentiful from Spanish galleons and other trading ships. This coast certainly had a history. No doubt about it.

"We've heard some Cancun stories. We've been coming here since 1983 and we've seen the growth. Even Playa del Carmen has grown."

"Playa grew because of the cruise ships," he told us. "First the cruise ships went to Cozumel, then to Playa, two days a week. That's what made Playa grow. Let's go back inside," Rodolfo said, moving towards the French doors. "I'll show you some lots for sale on the beach."

Back in his office, Rodolfo brought out a well-used topographical map of Puerto Morelos. He pushed aside a marble paperweight shaped like the reclining Mayan god, *Chac Mool,* and spread out the map, carefully unfolding creases as it covered the wide expanse of his expensive, mahogany desk. One of the advantages of living in a rain forest, I mused; you get your pick of hardwoods.

"Actually," he said, "the lot on my right is for sale, here on the beach. It is very buildable; thirty by thirty five meters."

We stared dumbly at each other as the realization sunk in: Mexico is on the metric system. If I had only known I'd be a land owner in Mexico one day, I would have paid more attention when studying tables of weights and measures in school. But converting meters to feet wasn't as difficult as it first seemed. One meter is just a smidgen more than three feet. We figured the lot to be ninety feet beach frontage by one hundred and five feet deep. A nice piece of property.

"What's the asking price?" Paul queried.

"Sixty thousand U.S., and that's very fair. It had been higher, but now, with the hurricane, prices are coming down."

That made sense as until the hurricane, every gringo in the world came down to Mexico between Christmas and Easter. The majority believed they wanted to buy a lot, build a house, and retire south of the border. And if that wasn't possible, well, there was always time share.

For a change, I thought, maybe our timing is right. It appeared that the hurricane had cooled off once hot Cancun . . . sellers were hungry.

"Will they take less than $60,000?" asked Paul as he shifted in his chair.

"I don't know," answered Rodolfo. "I also have another lot for sale with a house, but the house is in bad shape. The hurricane knocked it off its foundation and it's still there on the ground. It's two kilometers north of Morelos."

"Can we take a look at the lot next door?"

In moments we were on our way outside again, past the maid who had worked her way into the colonial kitchen and now stood before a sink full of dishes. Her *huipile,* the white embroidered dress of Mayan women still popular in the Yucatan, was so clean and starched, it looked as if she were ready to attend mass rather than tackle housework. I watched her lift a ceramic pot painted in the Talavera style high onto a shelf, and wondered, not for the first time, how do they do it?

When driving up and down the Quintana Roo coast, we often saw young Mayan girls coming out of the jungle from narrow dirt paths, marked by a stick with an empty soda or bleach bottle tied to it, dressed in the whitest, cleanest, prettiest Sunday dresses, with colorful ribbons carefully braided into their shiny hair. We knew many lived in small huts with dirt floors, probably had no running water, and in those days, definitely no electricity. So how *did* they do it? If cleanliness was next to godliness, they were spiritual beings for sure.

Rodolfo pointed out the boundaries of the lot next door—a bona fide beachfront lot. The beach was wide and the Caribbean sand white, but I felt it was too close to town. Nevertheless, here we were, not even one full day in Mexico and we had located a beachfront lot for sale.

"This is a nice lot," Paul began, as he turned in a three hundred and sixty degree circle, taking it all in, "but we'd also like to see the other lot. How do you get there?"

"Do you know the beach road out near *Cabañas La Ceiba*?" asked Rodolfo. "Take that road and continue past Crococun Road. Then drive another couple kilometers and you'll come to a tall house on a bay. It's next to that. The lot is $25,000 U.S. and it includes the house; there is no electricity yet, but some day it will come. Let me know if you like it," he finished.

"Well, thank you for your time. We appreciate your help and we'll get back to you after we see the lot. Oh, by the way, if we do buy a lot, who can build the house for us?"

"I'm a contractor and have built many homes here, including my own," he said as he motioned to the huge structure behind him.

"Okay, well, that's good to know. I guess we'll drive north of town and see you sometime tomorrow," Paul finished. "Thanks again."

Our first day in Puerto Morelos was proving to be a very good day for beachfront lots. Already we had two possibilities, and our vacation had barely begun. We walked to the car, climbed in. On the road . . . again.

———⟫◆⟪———

Rodolfo had pointed us north heading towards the beach road. We drove slowly down the half paved, half dirt street, taking in the town. In three blocks the pavement ended and so did the houses. Then the road became *sascab*. We maneuvered slowly, with caution, in one rut, out another, some so deep it seemed we were in up to the axels. Thank goodness it was dry. Small clouds of sand colored dust trailed behind us.

I marveled at the solitude of the jungle; it was uncharacteristically still. Although countless birds should have been singing, the hurricane had temporarily banned their songs. Birds couldn't live without trees for food and refuge. A friend told us how he'd almost caught a baby White-Fronted parrot on this road, but the bright green bird avoided capture, and flew back into the now barren jungle. It would soon die, he explained, as the forest couldn't sustain life until the foliage grew back.

Even without foliage, we knew this road; it was the road that led to Alejandro's house.

"We'll be going right by Alejandro's," Paul said as he adjusted the rear view mirror on our Volkswagen Beetle. VW was our vehicle of choice in Mexico; this car had many advantages in a third world country: you could give it a push start, if necessary; it had no radiator, so no overheating; and when gas was selling in expensive liters, well, you filled the tank and it almost seemed reasonable.

If only Mexico's car rental agencies were as user-friendly as the VW. *Qué lástima.* What a pity, they were not. We soon learned the rental agencies had their own special form of corruption, so we developed a rental agency ritual: we walked around the car with the agent and noted all dents and scratches before we were road-bound; we always checked for a spare tire in the trunk along with a jack; and we even read the contract and fine print *before* we signed it.

Who knew what ambiguous charges might creep into the final tally? We took full insurance—bumper to bumper—and made sure we had the agency's phone number, in case of emergency.

In the 1980s, if your flight arrived at night, no rental company would rent you a car. Just too many accidents occurred when gringos drove at night.

We heard horror stories about driving over the years, although things have now improved. We rented our first Mexican car in Merida from a Canadian travel agent who told us about a drunk gringo who drove into a crowd of people at a bus stop near Progreso on Christmas Eve, killing a young boy and maiming others. In Mexico, the law follows the Napoleonic Code, so one is guilty until proven innocent. The drunk driver was arrested and thrown into the town *carcel*, but had to be transferred to a different city that very night, as an angry mob circled the jail, threatening to lynch him. I don't know if the Canadian was just making light conversation or wanted to scare me to death by telling me this, but he succeeded in the latter. Two rules we keep to this day are: we avoid driving at night, and we never drink and drive in Mexico.

As he maneuvered the car with finesse, Paul said, "Good old Volkswagens, they can really take the dirt roads. Since we're going right by Alejandro's, we can see what's left of it."

"Karla said nothing was left," I replied as I brushed my hair off my neck, now damp from humidity.

The washboard road stopped our conversation as Paul concentrated on driving. We soon came to a familiar bend, and then we saw *Cabañas La Ceiba*. What a shock. The hotel's reception area and restaurant still stood, but they were in shambles, cracked through the middle. The once enchanting *cabañas* faired even worse: they were uprooted and a few stood straight on end, tossed about like children's building blocks. Gone, too, were the elegant, leggy coco palms, just as Karla said, and any tree left standing had been reduced to a mere stump, devoid of fronds—stubble. Any remaining brush was charred or burned, as if an unforgiving forest fire had ravaged the area. It was beyond ugly. It was desolate; it was sad.

After passing the ruined hotel we were even more curious about what might be left of Alejandro's house. Soon we recognized his wide stretch of beach and saw the veterinarian's house still standing, two doors down from Alejandro's. We'd been told everything had been destroyed on the beach, so it was a relief to see something. Then we saw Jacinto's *bodega,* the Mayan style pyramid dwelling Alejandro had built for the caretaker.

How odd that it was still standing. It looked rock solid, while in the place where Alejandro's house had been—absolutely nothing. Not a tree, no sign of a sea wall, no cement. Nothing to show a house had ever been there, that it had ever existed. It had disappeared.

I stared at stubby, *zapote* wood pilings in the water, once a part of the dock; heard the swoosh of a pelican as it dove into the water surprising an unsuspecting fish; gazed out at the Palancar Reef, watching waves curl, collide, recede. Just face it, I told myself. There is nothing left of Alejandro's magical Mediterranean style house. *Nada.*

Next to Alejandro's we saw his neighbor's house. It was a large modern-looking structure, two stories high, and apparently untouched. I blinked twice. Was this for real?

"Paul, look at Barry's house!" I pointed in surprise. "It looks like it survived the hurricane!"

"I can't believe it!" exclaimed Paul, as surprised as I was.

"How did he manage that?"

Barry was another local character, an American ex-pat and Los Angeles refugee. We'd met him at the bar at *Cabañas La Ceiba* whenever we stayed there. In fact, each time we were in the bar, so was Barry, having a stiff one, he told us. Obviously this was his home away from home. Although the bar was well-appointed, a knockout hardwood finished to a delicate sheen, with tall, comfortable bar stools curled underneath, Barry always stood at one end, kind of Matt Dillon style. Like a wrangler just in off the plains, he slouched into a comfortable position as he put back his daily dose of the hard stuff.

We got to know him on our recurring trips to Puerto Morelos. He was a fixture already and we were fast becoming fixtures at the *cabañas*. Eventually he'd invited us to see the house that now stood before us.

Barry had left Los Angeles a few years before, driving a classic Thunderbird and toting a long board, though he didn't look a surfer, along with his worldly second wife to the wild Mexican coast of Quintana Roo. They hardly seemed a match. She was years, maybe decades, younger than Barry and very Junior League. Exactly how she had become a player in this bizarre Mexico scenario was beyond me. Either quiet or aloof, she never spoke a word and seemed to have a sense of ennui about her Mexican experience.

Barry was the extreme opposite, not lacking in the personality department. It was a surprise to find someone in his late fifties, back in those days before luxury became synonymous with the Riviera Maya, brazen enough to give up a normal life in the States and traipse down to some little-known spot in the Mexican Caribbean to build a house. Tall and wiry, his hair was just beginning to thin when we met him, but no doubt he'd been a contender in his day. Although not handsome, he had a certain sexiness, and anything lacking in the looks department he made up for with his audacious nature. He was plainly funny—now thinking back on it, probably always drunk—and a natural showman. His previous profession as a plastics salesman had no doubt been well served by his king-of-the-hill mentality. When Barry spoke, everyone listened.

The night we met him he regaled us with wild stories about building a house in Mexico.

"The experience of a lifetime!" he kept repeating, his mantra at the time.

It immediately became apparent he'd had several high-profile run-ins with local law enforcement.

"If you see that sign in front of my house, "*Privada, no pasa,*" that does *not* mean you!" he bellowed. "That means those damn Mexicans! The little bastards!"

"But Barry," I protested in a teasing manner, "weren't they here first?"

"Screw 'em! They put me through hell. Pure, unadulterated hell! I had to let them know I meant it when I said "no trespassing." So, one night a few of them were walking on my lawn . . . my goddamn lawn, for Chris' sakes! Do you know how hard it *is* to grow a lawn here? How impossible it is to find *grass seed*? Oh, Christ," he shook his head remembering the peril of it all.

"Well, I came out with my Smith and Wesson and let them know I meant "*no pasa.*" That was my limit. They walked on my goddamn lawn!"

"Oh, my God! You didn't shoot at them, did you?" I asked.

His eyes widened and he pounded his fist on the solid wood bar. "Goddammit, no! But I should have. I've had it with this trespassing bullshit," he continued in a worked up manner.

"They had me arrested! Can you believe it? I had to spend the night in jail. They called the *federales* on me. Just because I had a gun! God damn them. Now I made the sign even bigger than before. Of course, they probably can't read English, the little bastards. Shit, what do I mean? They probably can't read Spanish!"

"You sound very upset. How long have you been down here?" I asked, guessing it was way too long.

"Three years. Three goddamn years. The experience of a lifetime. Ha! I've had it. There's no law. They make it up as they go along. They're out to get us gringos. It was torture—pure torture—to build my house. But I showed them; I finished in spite of it all.

"And it's one helluva house. Drop in sometime. We just finished six months ago."

As he spoke of his house, a peace came over him; once a troubled sea, he was now calm.

"We'd love to see it," I replied. "Next time we're walking by we'll see if you're home."

"Well, if I'm not at home, you can find me right here at this bar with Pedro, right, Pedro?"

Pedro didn't even have to nod in agreement. We knew Barry's routine by now. Day or night, he was at the bar at *Cabañas La Ceiba*. Happy hour or not-so-happy hour. Quite the fixture.

So this had been our introduction to crazy Barry and his L.A. style house. Paul pulled the car into the Mayan rock driveway, now littered with palm fronds, pieces of wood, cement, conch shells, window frames, and general storm debris.

"It's obvious no one is here," Paul said, getting out of the car. "Let's take a look." It was eerie being there and finding Barry's house after passing Alejandro's and seeing nothing but Jacinto's *bodega*.

"Let's walk to the beach and see how high the tide is," Paul suggested.

We picked our way through the rubble, climbing along carefully, and intently watching the ground as not to fall. Slowly we made our way to the beach.

"Oh, my God!" I gasped as we came alongside the two-story house. Paul stopped.

"What?" he yelled, turning back. "Oh, no!" he exclaimed, understanding my alarm. Looking at the side view of Barry's house, we could see why no one was there. The house had been ripped in half from the ocean-side, the backside. How it was still standing, I didn't know. It looked like a child's doll house, with no walls on the beach side—the side that now faced us—with the bare rooms exposed and open to the elements.

The hurricane had sheered off the entire back of the house and deposited it on the beach. There before us lay a mass of rebar, granite, marble, tile, windows, kitchen parts, cupboards, chairs, refrigerator door, enormous junks of cement, bed frames, banisters, various household items. And the huge, gaping hole from this skeleton of a house just yawned at us. Someone told us later the foundation had been destroyed by water surge, not wind. In a hurricane, the surge was the element that ravaged construction because it ate away at the foundation, eventually toppling the structure if the storm lasted long enough or stalled out over that location.

Most buildings cannot handle more than a few hours of continuous water surge. For this reason Rodolfo built a sea wall in front of his property twelve feet high with deep pilings, hoping the surge would first distress the pilings before reaching the house. In Rodolfo's case, he had been fortunate and this plan had worked.

"I can't believe it!" Paul said. "Look at this!"

We stared in disbelief at the wreckage. We were beginning to see how much devastation *Gilberto* had caused, now, in a very personal way. Alejandro's house had totally disappeared, but maybe this half a house was worse. Later, as stories circulated about the hurricane, we heard Barry's contractor had gone to see what damage *Gilberto* had done and had been as fooled as we had been.

Local rumor had it that after the storm subsided, he'd gone to Barry's with a friend, and on viewing the structure from the road had been pleasantly surprised that his work still stood. Then he walked to the front door, opened it with a key, and was hit with a dose of reality.

We heard later that, in spite of the ruined house, Barry had been lucky. Just three months before the hurricane he'd sold it for a cool $250,000 U.S., in a cash deal to an older couple. While his luck held, theirs failed miserably. Someone had told the new buyers, or so it was rumored, that house insurance in Mexico was costly, plus it might not pay off, should a disaster strike. So they never purchased house insurance. They only owned the house a matter of months and along came *Gilberto*. Supposedly they were devastated by this bad fortune, and had no desire to re-build. It was one of many stories we would start to hear about the hurricane, now that we were getting to know the locals.

"Let's walk over to Alejandro's," I said to Paul, grabbing his hand as if that would provide some form of reassurance.

We picked our way through the debris intermingled with sea grass, taking sideways looks at the house where we'd had drinks with Barry and his youthful wife. In the shallow Caribbean water, perched at a precarious angle, sat a mosque-like Arabian dome, formerly the focal point of Barry's stylized house. Still covered in small, cobalt-colored mosaics, it caught an occasional glimmer from the merciless sun, as if to prove its previous existence.

I thought back to the evening we had stopped in for the house tour. Surprisingly, Barry had been there and not at the bar. He had been in full Barry-form that night, showing off the expensive handmade Mexican tiles, the marble countertops, pointing out the finely crafted hardwood furniture made from stunning mahogany and a curious zebra-striped wood called *boem*. We'd marveled at the Arab-style dome, the cathedral ceiling, the number of bathrooms. We'd listened to the continuation of his contractor stories, how the man spoke no English, Barry spoke no Spanish, and the pandemonium that erupted daily due to these exchanges.

He told us how the price bounced about, depending on the peso and the fluctuating material costs for construction goods from week to week, but for the most part, his contractor had held to the original pricing structure. The timeline Barry had hoped for came and went, however, and the project dragged on into some Mexican twilight zone. Each day at 6 a.m., Barry said he awoke to the sound of chink-chink-chink. Tap, tap, tap. Chink-chink-chink. Tap, tap, tap. The Mayan workers were incredibly early risers and, as they lived on the site, at daybreak they started chipping and shaping the rocks they would use that day.

These stories filled my head for a moment, and then, reality. It was impossible for me to believe everything was gone. Barry's house was ruined. Now we were climbing through more debris from another familiar house, onto another familiar beach. Alejandro's beach. Where no trace—not a trace!—of Alejandro's house still stood. But stranger still, as we climbed through the wreckage, the day began to take on the feeling of a Corona ad. You know the one, where a tanned, buff gringo throws away his beeper, and declares he's found paradise on this white sand beach, as the camera zooms to a bucket of Coronas washed in surf, palms swaying in the background. It felt just like that.

Of course the debris was still there, but as I looked out at the water, the beauty of the day itself—that idyllic, breezy, sunny day there in the Caribbean, weather balmy—felt like paradise. Here we stood in Carthage, yet the sky was unbelievably blue and calm, merinque-shaped cumulus hung in the background. Staring out at the reef, I watched as the waves crested, hit the coral, and splayed a mist of water back into the turquoise sea. Pure ethereal beauty. It had to be God's cosmic joke. The day's total perfection seemed a sharp contrast to *Gilberto's* path of destruction.

"Jacinto's house is in good shape," Paul remarked, taking it in as we walked up the beach. "Look at it. It's like it hasn't been touched. Strange."

"It is weird," I agreed. "I wonder if Alejandro's house blocked the wind, or if the shape, like a Mayan pyramid, helped protect it."

"We'll never know," answered Paul. "Just one of those things. Like when earthquakes hit California. One person's house will be totally destroyed while the house next door won't have a broken coffee cup. Who can say why?"

Who could say why? It wouldn't be till years later that we heard a strange tale about Alejandro and his Mayan caretaker, Jacinto. Just weeks before the hurricane they'd had a vicious fight, Alejandro told us, and Jacinto had ended the argument by shouting a curse at him. A Mayan curse? Then Jacinto began a series of strange rituals—burning candles, lots of candles—and lighting copal, a Mayan incense with a pungent odor. Alejandro had been physically shaken by the encounter, but then, who wouldn't be unnerved at being the target of an angry Mayan's threats and curses? We could never put aside the coincidence, though, that Alejandro's house disappeared leaving no trace after the hurricane, and Jacinto's *bodega* in the shape of a Mayan pyramid still stood firm, only a few feet from where the main house had been.

Here we were in the land of the Maya. Perhaps a higher power was at work; maybe it was sheer coincidence or maybe Jacinto had enlisted the talents of a shaman to get even with Alejandro. Each *pueblo* had a local *bruja,* or witch, and every marketplace had a stall selling herbs and candles for rituals and magic. This practice was as common for a Mayan as filling a prescription was for me.

But in talking to friends who knew about these matters, they told me the state of the one being cursed, his receptivity, was the all important ingredient—the component *du jour.* If that person, the magic's target, felt at risk, then trickery could be done.

We didn't know if Alejandro was superstitious or not. But he told us about the curse. Perhaps he was a willing receptor, and Jacinto's curse found its mark. Or perhaps, because his house had a weak foundation and no sea wall, the wind and surge were just strong enough that day to blow his house into the sea and oblivion.

All in all, magic had failed not only Alejandro but the Caribbean coast during *Gilberto's* raging. It was hard to not be downcast about the total devastation. Now we knew firsthand that even paradise had its perils. More than once we thought about what would have happened to us if we had built our house before the hurricane. Would it have withstood the storm? Or would we be in the same sorry place with Alejandro? Maybe in some way it had been dumb luck to have first hooked up with him. All those years waiting, when we felt we'd been luckless, maybe luck had been with us after all. Maybe we'd been saved, at least for now, from the disheartening experience of building our dream house, only to see it taken by storm.

Many thoughts raced through my mind that day, but in the end, who could say? I was in the mysterious land of the Maya. All things were possible.

—————————>●●<—————————

We trekked to the rental car, and began driving north on the rural, *sascab* road. A strange quiet came over me; seeing so much devastation was numbing. I was shell-shocked from viewing *Gilberto's* wrath up close, and Paul was as thoughtful as I.

A slight Caribbean breeze offered a respite from the heat of the day as we slowly drove over and through the sandy ruts. A house across from Barry's was still standing, apparently another hurricane survivor.

Two lots north of Barry's a brand new condo complex with twelve units had recently been built. Like Barry's house, it was peeled in half, gaping open. Constructed just six months before the hurricane, it seemed an upscale addition to the neighborhood, sporting both a satellite dish and a pool. Now it stood as forlorn and empty as Barry's. We heard the owner was suing the contractor—a true Mexican standoff. The owner swore the complex had been demolished due to poor design and construction. I personally thought it had more to do with Mother Nature's revenge than with quality of construction. But one thing I *was* certain of: it would be light years before a Mexican court came to a decision on it.

"Just keep on driving," I said to Paul. "You can't look back."

There was certainly little that could be done to help the situation on the coast that day, or any day, immediately following the hurricane. I knew, however, that should we ever build a house in this incredibly beautiful area, buying house insurance would be first on my list of things to do. That was a fact.

Déjà Vu

Back on the bumpy beach road we passed the crossroads for Crococun, a "live" crocodile farm and zoo. Crococun housed a minimum number of reptiles before the hurricane, but now there were none, as every single snake and crocodile escaped during the storm. The reptiles residing at the zoo barely qualified as live animals. Hearing of their exodus, cartoon images of crocodiles on crutches, limping their way to the ocean, came to mind. When the force of nature freed them, all caged reptiles and snakes dashed towards the sea, reminiscent of some Paleozoic evolutionary survival pattern.

Along with the escape of the snakes, we heard a story about a local innkeeper, Ana Mario Almada, of Amar Inn, and how she had come back to town after evacuating like everyone else, only to find half of her *cabañas* torn to pieces. A striking woman in her sixties, she'd left central Mexico and resettled on the Quintana Roo coast to open a bed and breakfast in Puerto Morelos with the help of her husband.

In a moment of introspection, on viewing the destruction from *Gilberto*, she prayed for a sign. Should she stay or pull up stakes and leave this rustic fishing village, having arrived a couple years before the storm. With her home and hotel in dilapidated condition, she and her husband were invited to stay with a friend who lived near Crococun while repairs were being made. One day, as she walked downstairs to the backyard, she stepped on a *cuatro narices*, a small, deadly viper, known also as a four-noser. It bit her on the foot. She took another step, and landed on top of another *cuatro narices*, which also bit her. A bite by a *cuatro narices* is bad enough, but local lore said in fifteen minutes you would be dead without injecting the antidote, as the snake's poison worked rapidly.

In Chiapas, the poorest and least populated Mexican state, indigenous Mayans take precautions against snake bites by carrying a stick in their left hand and a machete in the right while clearing maize fields. The stick is used to bend back brush on the path in front of them so as to expose and ferret out snakes, especially the *cuatro narices*. Thus disturbed, the snake will then bite the stick, not the Mayan's hand, saving him from a fatal bite. Then with machetes, brush is cut and the land is cleared. To further ensure safety when far away from hospitals and antidotes, these field workers cut four-inch plastic PVC pipes in half, strapping them to their front legs with ropes from knee to ankle, for protection from the deadly *cuatro narices*, should a snake be missed on the first pass through the fields.

As Ana Mario grabbed her foot, she saw two Mayans a few hundred feet away. "Something bit me," she cried out.

The Mayans ran towards her. One held her by the arm, attempting to look at the injury, while the other ran through the brush looking for the snakes. Amazingly, the snakes were captured and identified. Charcoal was located and given to Ana Mario as a neutralizer for the venom. By this time her husband was at her side, and moments later a friend arrived and drove them to the small medical clinic in Puerto Morelos where she was given a shot of the anti-toxin.

Was the *cuatro narices* that bit Ana Mario a renegade from Crococun Zoo? No one knew, but her body was reacting to the bite and she continued to swell as the venom took hold. Their friend drove Ana Mario and her husband to Cancun, where one of the hospitals administered another shot for the venom. Then they drove her to Merida, two hundred miles away, for more advanced treatment. At the hospital in Merida, Ana Mario's body continued to swell, but the doctor told her husband she would make it. Lucky, he continued, that she was wearing *huaraches*, the Mexican sandal with tire-tread sole. Due to its thickness, the snakes only punctured her with two fangs rather than four.

Ana Mario's daughter, Ana Luisa, arrived in Merida the next day and waited for her mother to convalesce. A few days later, when Ana Mario was ready to be released from the hospital, Ana Luisa questioned her mother about the bite, asking if it was the sign she'd been waiting for.

"Yes," the woman responded, her voice still subdued from her ordeal. "I was given a sign."

"I agree," the younger woman told her mother in a serious tone. "The snake bites were enough to make us all want to leave this place."

"No, you don't understand," the recovering woman said, shaking her head. "The snake bite was the message that my place is here. Here is where I survived, and here is where I will stay."

Others may have viewed God's handiwork differently, but the innkeeper had been right about finding her place. Ana Mario Almada founded an ecological group, *Lu'um Ka'naab*, that fought to preserve the Palancar Reef (later renamed Great Mesoamerican Reef) the second largest coral reef in the world, which stretches just a half mile off Puerto Morelos' shore. Due to her and her daughter's hard-nosed perseverance, Puerto Morelos was named a national ecological park by the Mexican government in 1998. Through their efforts, the mangroves surrounding the town were also preserved, similar to a much publicized project in Florida's everglades. At present it is illegal to fill the mangroves in Puerto Morelos for building projects.

After cruising down the *sacsab* road for another ten minutes we located the second lot Rodolfo had told us about, but after a closer look, we decided we preferred his first choice and headed back to town.

That night we dined at *Posada Amor*, the old love-in *cabañas* and restaurant located on the town square. The local story was the owner had become infatuated with the hippie movement and had dedicated his *cabañas* to the concept of spiritual love. At one end of the white-washed dining room a small shrine had been erected. On a side buffet, heart-shaped rocks, carved wooden hearts, sand candles, shells, conches and black and white photographs of spectacular sunsets were displayed. Although the photos were faded with soft wrinkles at the corners and the handmade art was funky at best, the restaurant emanated a vibe from the days of peace and love. A time warp but with a Mexican twist, it was like stepping back into a kinder, gentler era of black light posters, Dylan songs, and love-ins.

As the inn's founder had departed this world, I guessed the shrine was not only a tribute to the concept of peace and love, but to *Posada Amor's* founder as well.

The hotel itself was a cluster of small *cabañas* with either bunk beds or hammocks. Screened windows, framed in local hardwoods, gave the rooms an airy feel, as long as the VEC ceiling fan, a staple in this tropical climate, was used in tandem. Turquoise tile floors, polished to a low luster, were impeccably clean. The units felt like a little colony, with shared bathrooms for some and private baths for others. Although it was all a cozy setup, quite close together, *Posada* was always full. With the cheapest price in town for a room, *Posada* had already established itself as a backpacker's paradise. The Euro crowd had embraced it, and even at this early date in the mid 80's, it was successfully on its way.

Since the founder's death, his wife and daughters, all Mexican beauties, plus their congenial brother, ran the establishment. Every morning and evening they set up a family table in one corner, showing a complete montage of the comings and goings of a very large, amiable group who shared in work, play, and meals. Paul and I watched, captivated by their interactions, surprised at how well they all got along. Part of the fun in eating at *Posada Amor* was not only the tasty regional cuisine, a lot of it fresh fish, but that for a time, you became an extension of this large, gregarious family.

———»•«———

At the hotel office the next morning, we asked the clerk if her husband, Rodolfo, was home. She said he'd gone to Cancun and asked what we needed. We told her we wanted to discuss both lots and the building project with him, and she suggested we see his partner, Joe Marino, since Rodolfo wouldn't be back until later that day.

"Have you seen the large, white house with the weather vane and rounded staircase?" she asked when giving us directions.

Paul and I looked at each other. In our many trips to Puerto Morelos over the years, we had often walked by this house and wondered about it. A Mayan style wall, made from chiseled, flat rocks, some rough, some smooth, set the compound apart from the other local houses. Peeking over the top of the stunning wall was the largest rubber tree I'd ever seen, with brilliant jade-colored leaves. The house even had a turret. Weird, for Maya Mexico.

Often we'd imagine who lived there, where they were from, what brought them to this small, Mexican fishing village in the middle of nowhere. Now, apparently, we would find out.

"Joe Marino?" Paul asked.

"Yes, Rodolfo and I have known him for many years. He and his family have been coming to Puerto Morelos for fifteen years. Even before we built the *cabañas* on the beach, they camped out at our site. He built his house, the large white one, right next to the Maya Meditation Center. Do you know where that is?"

I gave a slight nod. "Yes, but what a surprise. Meditation in Mexico?" I responded.

"Oh, meditation is very popular here, and so is yoga," the clerk assured me. Over the years, as we got to know Puerto Morelos, we noticed it had a cosmic draw for artists, psychics, healers, and occasionally, the offbeat traveler. In time, a second meditation center opened, cornering the market on time travel, followed by yoga studios, massage and healing centers, a goddess center and art shops. Then would come aura readers, drummers, jungle journeyers, and Maya calendar devotees. Even being way down south in Mexico, we still captured the cosmic crowd. New age philosophies crept into the workings of the town and flourished. We were a speed bump, a *tope*, in the road to spiritual enlightenment for many.

Why Puerto Morelos? What was the attraction, the spiritual thread connecting this spot to meditation groups, yoga centers, new age healers?

A modern Maya goddess explained it to me this way: for over a millennium, the Maya women used this coastal port as a place to congregate before journeying to the island Cozumel, which was considered a fertility site blessed by the goddess *Ixchel*. *Ixchel* was the moon goddess in the Mayan pantheon, married to her consort, *Itzamna*, Lord of the Heavens. She was also patroness of pregnancy, according to archeologist Sylvanus Morley.

In *The Ancient Maya*, Morley wrote the Maya greatly desired children and loved them deeply. Women even "asked them of idols with gifts and prayers." And to induce pregnancy, a woman placed the image of *Ixchel*, goddess of pregnancy and childbirth, under her bed.

So for eons, Puerto Morelos was a gathering spot for women awaiting passage to Cozumel to honor the goddess *Ixchel*. From the shores of Puerto Morelos their spiritual journey began. No doubt it was a place where incantations had been chanted. It had drawn ancient Mayans here, and even now, the goddess said, it was pulling others with a spiritual craving to its shores.

How appropriate that we should land here, I thought. Even though I'd put my meditation mode on automatic pilot when I joined the ranks of the seriously employed in San Francisco, finding my spiritual place in the world had always been a primary focus in my adult life. Making money had happened almost as a sideline, but it afforded me the gift of being here, in this spot, now.

———>●<———

We rang the bell positioned under a brass plaque reading Villas Marino, next to a double garage with doors crafted out of the most beautifully striped Mexican hardwood I had seen yet. The wood was dark as coffee beans, but with a wide, ivory stripe throughout, almost zebra-esque in pattern. Only in Mexico, I mused, are garage doors so achingly beautiful I want to caress them. It said something about the level of craftsmanship in Mexico, along with the tremendous amount of natural resources available in this country. Men here oftentimes learned a trade from their fathers, so artisans came from a long line of others who had done the very same thing. The work was in their blood. It had to reflect on the workmanship—in the beauty and pride reflected in a finished piece—as if a long line of forefathers smiled from some lofty spot on high at the completion of every project. Here in Mexico, it was not uncommon to personally know the man who built your house, or made your cupboards, or painted your handmade tiles. Mexico still brought you back to the roots, the beginning of things.

At that moment, the door swung open and we were face-to-face with a man of medium build, blond hair, probably in his thirties. No doubt about it, definitely American.

"Hi, we're looking for Joe Marino," Paul began. "The clerk at Hotel Paradise told us he could help us out."

"I'm Joe Marino, Junior. My father, Joe Senior, worked with Rodolfo for years, but he's semi-retired now and I'm picking up a lot of the construction work. Why don't you come in," he said, smiling as he waved us into the entryway of the compound.

Walking through that doorway, I later realized, seemed to be the bridge between the world of almost owning land in Mexico, and finally realizing a land buy. From that point on, things seemed to move in the right direction.

We told him who we were and explained our desire for a beachfront lot and the need for a contractor and how his father's company had been highly recommended.

"I know of another beachfront lot for sale," Joe Marino said, "if you haven't decided yet on what you've already seen. It's half a mile north, near the ruins of *Cabañas La Ceiba*. Do you know the spot?"

"Yes, we do," I answered, thinking how odd it was that he called *Cabañas La Ceiba* a ruin, but in actuality, it certainly was. "The beach is nice there, very quiet. Where, exactly, is the lot and how large is it?"

"It's just north of the *cabañas*, with one hundred feet of beach frontage, thirty-some meters, and actually, there's a hitch. There's a house already on the property, but it was devastated by the hurricane."

"Do you know who the house belongs to?" Paul asked.

"Yes, an older couple just bought it from a guy from L.A." Joe replied.

Paul shot me a glance. "Wait a minute. That wasn't Barry's old house, was it?"

"As a matter of fact, yes. Did you know Barry?" Joe asked, now curious.

"I can't believe it! We knew Barry and the guy next to him, Alejandro. This is too weird," I said, shaking my head.

"I seem to have struck a nerve somehow," Joe said, giving us a quizzical look. "The lot is for sale. The people who now own the house are friends, or acquaintances, of ours. They paid a hefty price for it, then two months later, *Gilberto*. They're not up to rebuilding, so they plan to sell."

"How much are they asking?" Paul wanted to know.

"Sixty thousand U.S." Joe responded. "It's worth it. It's a nice lot."

"Can you get in touch with them. I think we'd like to make an offer," Paul said, as he eyed me and smiled.

"I'll call them tonight. You can check back tomorrow and I'll have more information for you. Will you be looking for a contractor? That's what I do," Joe indicated with a nod that we should take a look at the luxurious surroundings and added, "Would you like a house tour?"

"Sure," I smiled in response as my heart did somersaults.

If I understood this right, Barry's lot, right next to Alejandro's, was for sale. We might be buying a lot right next to the house that first brought us to Puerto Morelos. Full circle. Completion of a cycle, I felt as if I'd just stepped into the second act of a play I'd written and was starring in. All my lines were perfect.

Joe began the house tour by leading us through a lush, tropical courtyard complete with bird cages encasing parrots, toucans, macaws. A serene swimming pool, its bottom a turquoise-blue mosaic, looked inviting. I felt like jumping in, to celebrate the elation I was feeling, and to cool off. At the edge of the pool, a male peacock took stock of us, intruders to his paradise. Surprisingly, we seemed more out of place than he did. The setting was so luxurious, having a peacock on the premises didn't seem unusual.

A large dragonfly skimmed across the pool, hesitating slightly as it tipped its double wings, then shot past the diving board and was gone. Areca palms, clumped near a screened breezeway, caught a rare breath of wind, their fronds swaying lightly. I saw a drab, little sparrow peck at birdseed outside the cage of a regal African Grey, who eyed him carefully from his perch.

"This is beautiful," I whispered. "And peacocks. Very lush."

"We do what we can," Joe said, smiling. "Glad you like it." He was enjoying the tour, and we were feeling comfortable with this newly discovered contractor. We talked to Joe a little longer, still numb from the fact that we might be buying a beachfront lot right next to Alejandro's, next door to the place we first set foot in Puerto Morelos over five years ago.

A great deal had happened since our first exposure to this little fishing village: we'd almost been Mexican land owners in Playa del Carmen; watched the government seize that land by eminent domain; then purchased—or more accurately—transferred that collateral into another beach lot north of *Capitán Lafitte* in an enormous parcel with rivers and *cenotes*. Then along came the hurricane of the century, blowing away every vestige of our project manager's house, putting everything connected to him in indefinite limbo.

Within twenty-four hours after landing in Mexico in pursuit of our backup plan, we'd met two contractors. Now one of them was telling us Barry's beach lot was for sale. And this quest for land all began with our desire to return that yellow umbrella, so long ago. It certainly seemed we were meant to be in Puerto Morelos.

"I'll give those people a call later," Joe's voice broke into my thoughts, "and see if they still want to sell."

"I hope so," Paul said. "Do you want us to stop over tomorrow morning and see if you were able to reach them?"

"Sounds good. I'll be here all morning. Well," he paused, "it's been nice meeting you both. Maybe we can work something out."

"I hope so," I replied, echoing Paul's remark. "Thanks so much for the house tour. It's a lovely place. *Hasta luego.*"

And with that, Paul and I walked out the door, into a blazing Mexican sun, full of hope and brimming with excitement, ready to begin yet another new chapter in our Mexican land adventure. Would we never give up?

"Paul," I spoke his name loudly, just under a shout. "I cannot believe it!"

"If it all works out, it will be unbelievable," Paul agreed. "That lot would be perfect for us. It's beautiful out there. Let's go check it out right now. Want to take a ride?"

As the VW bug puttered down the dusty, *sascab* road, I realized we may be driving to our new land—the land that crazy Barry's demolished house was on. Was I naïve enough to think things might work out for us this time?

Maybe, for once, we were in the right place at the right time. And maybe we'd be dealing with someone who was willing to work with us. Joe Marino seemed reasonable, helpful. Were our fortunes shifting? Or were we setting ourselves up for the biggest letdown yet?

We arrived at Barry's old house and parked in what was left of the driveway. As I climbed out of the car, I watched a magnificent frigatebird catch a thermal high above us, tip its wings, and soar off into an enormous sky. Then my gaze shifted to the house, the unflattering remnant of someone's Caribbean dream.

"Oh, this poor house. What an ordeal it's been through. I can hardly believe everything we've heard today. I feel sorry for the couple who bought this place three months before the hurricane. It's almost inconceivable what's happened to them. I can understand wanting to call it quits."

"Yeah, it is too bad," Paul murmured as he took a look around.

"This is an exceptional lot, excluding the half demolished house, of course. This end of town is much nicer than the south end. Down there you have the dock, the ferry, all the trucks lined up on the road. The north end is definitely quieter."

"Alejandro picked a good spot," I agreed. "And even though there are other houses around, they're far enough apart so it doesn't feel closed in, like that lot in town did."

"It seems like a good deal. We would have wider beach frontage, but if we buy it, we'll have to demolish the remains of the house before we build. So we'd be looking at that as an additional expense. Probably not that much though, here in Mexico.

"The only thing I don't like about it is *that*," and he pointed to the now ruined condo complex just north of us. It was an unsightly mountain of rubble.

"Well, won't that be cleaned up, or rebuilt?" I asked.

"We'll ask Joe tomorrow. But you know how slow things can go in Mexico," Paul replied.

We walked around the building and the debris, commenting on what we remembered of the house: the tile, the kitchen, the Arabian dome—now lying cockeyed in the ocean, and the garage, which was still standing.

"I love it out here, Paul. It's so calm, and I like the fact that it was our first introduction to Puerto Morelos. I mean, if this all comes together, we'll be right next to Alejandro's old house. What are the odds of that happening? After all the run-around we had—for five years! And now, possibly buying the lot right next door. And his house was devastated by the hurricane . . . gone."

"Yes, it's weird all right. But it's not a done deal yet. There are still things to be discussed and we have to make sure they're selling."

"That's right. It could just be a pipe dream," I added. But what a pleasant dream it was. Who would ever have known, when we climbed into that rusty, yellow Honda five years ago on the Cobá road, that we would end up in Puerto Morelos, buying a lot right next door to Alejandro's house, when he was telling us those wild, Yucatan tales?

Walking on Sunshine

A rooster's crow awakened us early the next morning and we bolted out of bed, anxious to test our newfound luck. We headed straight for Joe Marino's and waited in quiet desperation after ringing the bell at his gate, knowing within a few minutes our fate would be sealed. Was the lot still for sale, or already sold? Soon, Joe answered the bell, wearing a smile.

"Well, hello. Look who's here," he said. "Come in. I have good news for you."

The cloud of uncertainty lifted, and I replied, "Thank goodness."

"You sound happy. How 'bout a cup of coffee while I go over details?"

We followed him into the screened patio past the caged birds. The peacock sunned itself at the pool's edge, barely acknowledging our entrance. A light dew covered the soft, green grass beneath the coco palms in the adjoining garden. I took a seat at the breakfast table. A Mexican-style tablecloth, with brilliant, blue embroidery on elegant white linen, matched the cushions on the rattan chairs across from me.

Over coffee, he told us the lot was still for sale, and the price was firm. We could call the sellers, get started on the sale of the property, and then begin the paperwork for our *fideicomiso*. He used a notary/attorney in Merida who could set things up for us. Notaries in Mexico have much more authority and education than U.S. notaries. They have law degrees and are authorized to license land transactions.

In the meantime, we discussed house plans and how to proceed with construction once all paperwork was finalized and we had the *fideicomiso* in hand. In Mexico, construction loans did not exist as interest rates were ridiculously high—about forty percent. The way to build in Mexico, he explained, was to estimate the total construction cost, set up a schedule with the contractor, and make deposits to a construction account on a monthly basis. Then the contactor could create his own timetable, order materials as needed, and hire workers for each aspect of the job.

We agreed to overnight express Joe a set of house plans once we returned to the U.S. so he and his engineer could give us a construction estimate and timeline. We figured one year would allow us enough time to pay for the project.

Joe poured me another cup of coffee. It was a dark, Mexican roast—delicious—with a hint of cinnamon. He said, "After you call the sellers and get a confirmation, why not go to Merida and see the notary, Reynoldo Garcia. He just finished the *fideicomiso* for the sellers, and you can get a jump on the paperwork, maybe give him signatures now. That way, after you pay for the lot, everything will be on file and you can save yourselves another trip to Mexico."

"Let's call the sellers, get their confirmation, then give the notary a call and and set up an appointment," Paul agreed, adding, "Maybe we can drive to Merida tomorrow."

"Sounds good," I agreed. "Can we call them now, Joe?"

"Of course, let's do it," he responded. Within a few minutes Paul was on the phone to the U.S., firming up our dream deal on Mexican property.

As he put down the receiver I asked, " Are we finally going to own a beachfront lot?" He was smiling, so I was certain all had gone as expected.

"Yes. They want to sell and have accepted our offer. Now we just need to make an appointment with your notary for tomorrow afternoon. What was his name?"

Joe moved towards the phone, then after rifling through a desk drawer, he located a small phone book and started dialing, "Reynoldo Garcia," he said. "Believe me, you will never forget it once you've met him."

Where was this efficiency coming from? I wondered. Within five minutes, Joe had more good news.

"Reynoldo has time tomorrow afternoon, around 1 p.m. He said he'll be glad to meet with you. He's at Bancomer on *Paseo de Montejo*. It's an easy location to find; then stay overnight in case he has more papers for you to sign the next day. You'll like him, plus he speaks English. He's a bit of a character and he has always done a fine job for us. He's worked on *fideicomisos* for everyone here in Puerto Morelos. You'll be in good hands, and ahead of schedule, something rarely accomplished here in Mexico," he smiled and gave us a knowing look.

Within a matter of twenty-four hours, we had accomplished what had not been done in more than five years with Alejandro. We were getting a *fideicomiso*, a Mexican title for land. But what was different about then and now? Were we more ready for it now? Or did good things truly come to those who waited? God knows we had fulfilled *that* end of the bargain.

Right then, a calm came over me. Things were falling into place, and at last, it was no longer necessary to question why.

———⟫•⟪———

So that's how it finally came together on our Mexican land adventure. As we sped through Mayan villages on our way to Merida, I took stock of the local countryside. Even though we were very near Cancun, a tourist metropolis, the back roads showed no evidence of its wealth, nor the modern-day conveniences we took for granted. In many ways, it was as if we stepped back in time, feasibly hundreds of years, with the exception of cars and the occasional electric pole.

Pigs and chickens ran everywhere, leading free-range lives in this Maya outback. *Palapa* huts made from *chit* trees, bound together with rope, floors of packed dirt, stood humbly amidst unplanned gardens of coco palms, lemon and orange trees. In between the small *pueblos*, occasionally a larger town would pop up, like Chemax or Valladolid.

These were characterized by a well-kept *zócalo*, town square, with a center garden and the ever-present church, cornerstone of civilization and culture. Charming and inviting as these places were, we hurried through them with uncharacteristic haste, as we had a date with destiny . . . or at least with a notary. We were one step closer to legally owning land in Mexico. We'd found someone who would help us create our title.

As we neared Merida we realized what a large city it was for the Yucatan—one million population. Extremely narrow streets were common—most one way—and the pace was hectic, both for driving and for walking. We marveled at the number of people in this colonial Yucatecan city. Checking the map, we located *Paseo de Montejo*, the grand boulevard set in motion at the turn of the century when Parisians had come to Merida to manufacture Panama hats.

The Victorian architecture on the wide boulevard was vaguely reminiscent of European cities, and when we located Reynoldo's bank building, we were pleased to find it was a converted mansion, now the environs of the working stiff, no longer home to the nouveau riche.

We entered through heavy Spanish style doors, and waited

for the secretary to assist us.

"Reynoldo Garcia?" I asked, trying hard to roll my "r's."

The petite secretary, her aquiline profile revealing her Mayan heritage, asked us to take a seat and we settled into two large easy chairs, belonging more in someone's living room than in an attorney's office. In the Yucatan, we noticed that office furniture had yet to be discovered, for no matter what type of office—be it bank, insurance firm or government building—all furniture looked out of place. These offices sported Scotch plaid couches with American Heritage wooden arm rests, and nicked coffee tables ready for TV dinners. Just another cultural tradition—house furniture in an office setting—that let you know how far from corporate America you were.

The converted mansion had twenty-foot ceilings and grand picture windows. Outside I watched a group of school girls in uniform—navy skirts and starched, white blouses—skip across the center median as a dilapidated, green city bus, brakes squealing, took a tight turn, its load of weary passengers leaning into it with practiced poise. A hammock vendor set down his cargo and wiped the sweat from his brow with a colorful scarf before re-adjusting his own Panama hat and heading back towards the main plaza.

Horse-drawn *calesas*, or carriages, ambled by, the smallish, overworked animals wearing dark blinders, pulling loads much too large, their ribs straining with the burden.

Inside the office we sat in air-conditioned coolness. The marble floor was well-polished and the secretary's desk sat on a dais, dead center. An oriental rug that had seen better days adorned the floor beneath her desk. I picked up a Spanish magazine and nervously paged through it. I didn't know what to expect of Reynoldo, nor with this meeting, for that matter. Both Paul and I were a little tense after the long drive, so to calm ourselves we made quiet small talk while we waited.

In a few minutes a slender man in a dark, European-cut business suit came rushing through the reception area. His most noticeable feature, sadly, was his hair—distinguishable because of a very bad hair weave. It looked like tiny little tufts of hair had been planted on his head in rows. Oh, dear, I cautioned myself. But his disposition made up for the weave. He radiated an odd charisma, and called out loudly, as though we were long lost friends, "Pablo and Juanita!"

"*Si*," we responded in unison.

"I am Reynoldo Garcia," he announced, as though he were addressing a party of Royals. We stared at him in surprise. "And yes, I speak excellent English!" This was said with a flourish.

"Hello, pleased to meet you," Paul answered.

I offered him a wide smile as we all shook hands. I already liked this fellow, and I had only moments ago met him.

For me, one of the joys of Mexico was the people. Everyone we met was so genuine, so very happy to be of service. No hidden agendas. What a refreshing change.

"I spoke with Joe Marino yesterday. He said you're planning to buy the beachfront property in Puerto Morelos. Nice land. What a pity about the hurricane."

"Yes, very bad luck," said Paul.

"But maybe things will work out better for you," he replied.

He did know how to say the right thing.

"Please, come this way. I'll show you to my office. I've had my secretary pull the *fideicomiso* files. Although Joe said you still have to finalize finances, you wanted to prepare as much as possible while you are here in Mexico. No problem with that at all," he spoke quickly while ushering us into his office.

"Here, have a seat. I was just getting ready to have lunch. Would you like to join me in Chinese food this afternoon?"

Reynoldo asked, a little smirk twisting the corners of his mouth.

"Chinese?"

"Yes, yes. We are very civilized here in Merida. Haven't you noticed? This city is very continental. It always has been; but you've no doubt heard the stories about the Parisians, and the *Paseo de Montejo*?" he whisked his arm outward, extending it towards the grand avenue just beyond the window.

"Yes, of course," Paul answered.

"The Yucatan has always been known for its cuisine; it's considered the best in Mexico, and not only by us Yucatecans. Have you tried it?"

"Definitely," Paul replied. "We've been to Merida a few times and enjoy it."

"Thank you, thank you," said Reynoldo, now bowing. "So glad you like it. Yes, the French added their touch by introducing European cuisine and architecture. Both have remained, even though the French have departed, but because of this continental influence, it is not unusual to find a variety of restaurants in Merida. And this Chinese restaurant I mentioned is exquisite! I know the chef personally and he does a superb job. Come, we must try it. Gabriella!" he shouted.

"We are going to lunch," he said in Spanish. "Have the files ready for Pablo and Juanita in two hours when we return, all right?" Gabriella nodded and watched him whisk us out the doorway we had barely walked into.

"Come," he instructed, "my car is parked around back. Oh, it is so good that I can practice my English. Now where are you from? Did Joe tell me you're from California?"

"Yes, San Francisco," Paul answered.

"A lovely city. Lovely. I had a wonderful trip to San Francisco many years ago. I always wanted to return. Maybe some day."

Paul said, "We have great restaurants in San Francisco, too.

And it *is* a beautiful city. I've done my share of traveling and it compares with the best of them."

"Definitely," replied Reynoldo, with conviction. "You are right! It is fantastic!" We were driving back towards the center of Merida, but were still on *Paseo de Montejo.*

"So, you want to live in Mexico?" Reynoldo asked.

"Yes, we do," I replied. "We both love this country. It's so tranquil compared to the United States, and the people here are very friendly. We love the ocean, and we especially love the little town, Puerto Morelos. It's such a different pace from the U.S., and it's safer here. Not so many guns. In the U.S., everyone has a gun, and there's so much violence, especially in cities."

"I agree, a lot of violence there. I see it in the newspapers. It must be a very dangerous place to live. Do you know why?"

Paul fielded this question. "The gun laws are extremely loose, even though they say they're trying to tighten them. There's barely a waiting period to buy one, and lobbyists work continuously to keep it that way. We don't feel safe in the States. People shoot each other driving on the freeway during morning rush hour. We feel much safer here in the Yucatan, although Mexico City may be another story."

"Well, if you don't make enemies with the military, you're fine here," Reynoldo said, "and staying away from Mexico City isn't a bad idea, either."

"Do many people have trouble with the military?" I asked.

"Only those of us in politics," he chuckled. "If you're not a supporter of the PRI [Partido Revolucionario Institucional], and if you become vocal, you can have problems here with the military *and* the police. I'm in the PRI, but I do not agree with its theories. They need to change; they need to wake up to the twentieth century, since we are almost through with it."

"You're involved in politics? With the PRI?" Paul continued.

"Yes, and I'm becoming more involved each day. I'll be making my first speech this weekend at a rally. I'm in what is considered the militant left wing of the party. We are not well-liked, by anyone, at this point, but we firmly believe change is necessary to improve our country.

"The PRI has been in power for sixty years, since 1929, here in Mexico, and it has created a single party system. Sure, you can say there is PAN [National Action Party] and also PRD [Partido Revolucionario Democratico]. But really, they are nothing. They'll never win an election, although Cuahtemoc Cardenas would have been the true winner of the 1988 election if Carlos Salinas had not rigged the votes. Cardenas was winning; everyone knew it, but never before has someone not chosen by the outgoing president become our next president. It is called, *el dedazo*, the finger. The Mexican president points at the next in line, and he then becomes his successor."

"I've read that recently, in *Newsweek*, I think," I interjected.

"Probably so," agreed Reynoldo, "it has been getting a lot of press lately. But back to Cardenas. He is the son of one of Mexico's most popular presidents, Lazaro Cardenas, who was president from 1934 to 1940, and the people of Mexico have a long memory. You don't mind a little history lesson, do you? Now that you will soon be landowners here in Mexico?"

We both shook our heads, amazed at his command of information and his willingness to discuss it with us.

"Lazaro Cardenas saw what was happening with the foreign-owned oil companies. They were robbing us of all our profits, taking land that the oil was on and giving nothing back. They were above the law, and above being taxed. Cardenas saw this," he continued, "so he nationalized the oil company; now the entire gasoline industry is run by the government. You know, Pemex, all the gas stations. Cardenas made it better for the people of Mexico.

"He also divided large tracts of privately owned land and distributed them to the peasants; much of Mexico's population is dirt poor, you know. He was the last president who helped the people. His son still has some of that fight in him, and the people remember. They will always remember the name Cardenas. Yes, Salinas had *el dedazo*, but he was also hand picked by powerful players in the corporate and political world from America, where he was educated."

"Didn't he attend Harvard?" I asked.

"Yes, a Harvard graduate. Salinas and his party, the PRI, did not plan to lose; would not lose. Not yet, anyway. So I am disillusioned by my own political party, but what can I do?" His question was rhetorical. "No other party is elected, so I must make changes within my own party in order to be heard. Is any of this making sense?"

I couldn't believe it. Here I was in Mexico, meeting a radical liberal, and he turns out to be our attorney. Who wrote this script? Abbie Hoffman?

"Well, this is all incredible. They rigged the ballot boxes?" I asked. "Carlos Salinas stole votes in the 1988 election?"

"Of course, of course. Nothing is beyond the PRI. But it will not always be this way. Why, most people in this country cannot even read! And do you know what the unemployment figures are? They will not even publish them because they are so shameful. In this country, with almost ninety million people, perhaps fifty percent can read. It's pitiful! Shameful!" he said, as he worked himself into a cold sweat.

"The people here will have another revolution if this continues," Reynoldo insisted.

In retrospect, his words rang true. The Chiapas Incident occurred New Year's Day, 1994, shortly after the ratification of

NAFTA (North American Free Trade Agreement). During the four-day clash of PRI against Zapatista National Liberation Army, one hundred were killed including military, guerillas, and wealthy land owners.

In Chiapas, land owners had been forced to deed back land originally granted by the government to the state's indigenous people, the Lacandon Mayans, who are Mexico's poorest people. Current statistics show these Maya earn approximately $200 U.S. dollars per year, and to supplement their earnings, they work the land granted them by the government. Half of all titled land in Mexico was bestowed through land grants, known also as *ejidos*.

Over the years, the Lacandones were pushed into smaller and more marginal areas for farming, as local ranchers required more land for the burgeoning cattle industry.

The ranchers appealed to the governing PRI party, and had the land grant usage overturned. With these new restrictions, the Lacandon Maya found it difficult to eke out a living. Ironically, these were the very conditions that pushed the Yucatec Maya into the Caste War of the Yucatan, which began in 1847 and continued sixty years, well into the twentieth century.

The Mayan's losing battle for their stolen land, plus the passage of NAFTA, which many in Mexico believed would further push the Mexican poor into an even lower economic strata, became the Zapatista guerillas' battle cry.

Sub-Comandante Marcos, leader of the freedom fighters, is still at large. Believed to be a university professor of philosophy, rumor has it that the man comes from a wealthy background. After releasing most of the hostages, Marcos and a group of his followers escaped to the Chiapas jungles, where it is said he still lives in hiding. Occasionally, he makes a televised statement claiming his distrust in the present government of President Vicente Fox, PAN.

In March, 2001, Marcos led a country wide march from Chiapas to Oaxaca to disclaim the new policies of President Fox. The march turned into a circus-like parade that lasted for days and covered thousands of miles. Marcos wears a ski mask to hide his identity when giving press conferences to the media. In Palenque, the heart of the Lacandon Maya, street vendors sell tiny Marcos dolls, the size of a clothespin, complete with ski mask and submachine gun.

As Reynoldo predicted years before it happened, a revolution was in the offing. Surprisingly, Fox's PAN overturned the decades-old PRI party's stronghold on Mexican politics in 2000. At this writing, Marcos has three demands he requires of the Fox presidency, and plans to hold out on peace agreements until those are met. Marcos is still at large.

"Here we are at the restaurant. Let's go inside," Reynoldo announced as he pulled the car into a parking lot next to a rambling, Victorian-style mansion.

It looked like quite the place, and I was a little embarrassed that I wasn't dressed as stylishly as the décor suggested. But what did I know? I was only a tourist from Cancun, and up to a day before, I had no idea I'd be meeting attorneys, notaries, and bank officials on this Mexican junket; at least not so soon.

As we traveled through Mexico over the years, I discovered the colonial cities tended towards conservative, traditional styles and values. In Merida, for instance, dress was not as casual as in Cancun. Women in Merida dressed very formally, wearing skirts and dresses, whereas in Cancun, women wore jeans and shorts. Beachwear was the norm on the coast.

On entering the dining room, a maitre d' immediately appeared, and from the kitchen, as if on cue, a chef came scurrying our way. Glad tidings of "Reynoldo" rang throughout the room. He introduced us as his guests of honor from San Francisco, "one of the world's finest cities."

With Reynoldo, everything was in superlatives. I loved his exuberance, his intellect, and his left wing leanings.

After the initial rush, Reynoldo instructed us to take a seat near the window.

"This is a lovely table, with a charming view of *Paseo de Montejo*. Let's take a look at the menu, then I will call over Raul. He'll suggest what to order, and we'll have a true Chinese feast. You can pretend you're in Hong Kong, not Merida," he kidded.

It was a strange sojourn, being in this Yucatecan city with a passionately left-of-center liberal, dining in a high-end Chinese restaurant and being served by a Mayan chef named Raul. What next? Lunch was a glorious feast, and believe me, we were fussed over. It was difficult to get up from the table and move onto the next event of the day: our *fideicomiso*.

We pulled behind Reynoldo's office building into the parking lot, quickly got out of the car and approached the office. Inside, the place was buzzing. Lots of late afternoon activity—no siesta break here. Again, we were ushered into Reynoldo's office and asked to take a seat. He walked out to his secretary's desk, and promptly returned with an overstuffed file, brimming with papers. Gabriella had been busy in our absence.

"Here's the document from the owners. Why don't you relax for a while. This will take me a half hour. Then I'll need your signatures."

Time passed slowly, but we amused ourselves with people watching. True to his word, Reynoldo returned with more papers in a half hour. The stack he held was quite impressive—a good thirty pages of legalese.

"This will be your complete copy of the *fideicomiso*, once you and the owners sign it. We'll have you sign now, and I have another copy for them to sign. I'll give you that copy tomorrow around noon. You can take it to the States with you and send it to them. Instruct them to sign it, and then it will all be legal. Once this is done, overnight express this material to me and I will have the original documents prepared and sent to our Cancun office for you to pick up. Then you will be legal property holders on record for the lot in Puerto Morelos. See, I told you it wouldn't be too difficult."

It did seem easy, with Reynoldo in our court. And Joe Marino. People who were working for us and treating us as valued clients. What a turnaround from what we had experienced with Alejandro.

We thanked Reynoldo and walked out of the Bancomer office in somewhat of a daze. The rush of hot air accompanied by the blinding Yucatan sun jolted me out of my trance.

"Reynoldo is a cross between Hunter Thompson and Ricardo Montalban," I told Paul.

"Good description. He's certainly efficient. Shall we head over to the Trinidad Hotel and get settled before our celebration dinner?"

I quickly agreed and off we went to the Trinidad.

———≫●≪———

The next day we returned to Reynoldo's office and found everything ready, just as he promised.

"There is one thing I must explain," Reynoldo said, a conspiratorial look crossing his face,"because of this situation with you and the present owner. I re-wrote a portion of the *fideicomiso* which will protect you once they've signed it."

"What situation?" I asked. "Why do we need protection?"

"It's a protection clause that says the land is already yours," he announced in a matter of fact tone, as if it were a fait accompli.

"What do you mean? The land isn't ours *yet*, Reynoldo!" I protested. "We still have to pay them. You know, *dinero*?"

"Not to worry, not to worry!" he exclaimed. "It will not hurt them. This is simply additional protection for you, because *of course* you are going to pay them. Just look at this as your protection while the process takes place. If they decide, after they receive the money, not to sign over the lot, then they would have both your money and the lot. And then nothing could be done. I have grown fond of you. I don't want anything to happen that might jeopardize you."

In retrospect, I should have realized that Reynoldo had already dealt with the property owners and had assessed them; we had not. Of course we assumed they were straight shooters like ourselves. In his own inimitable way, he was trying to save us from something that could have been irrevocable.

It was an odd reversal. We were enroute from having no safeguards at all with Alejandro, to having more protection than a mafia don's daughter.

"Listen, don't worry about it," he added. "This is all written in Spanish. Just tell them to sign it. You know you are honorable. You will uphold your end of the bargain. You will pay them. This is, simply . . . how do you say it in English?" he searched for the phrase. "Ah, yes! This is your ace in the hole. They will never know what it says and it is simply your insurance policy. My gift to you. I don't want you to lose money, and besides that, I don't have time right now to re-write it."

There it was, the practical side of the matter. Reynoldo had taken it into his own hands to write the document as he saw fit. This was just the beginning. We soon realized this was the way things were done in Mexico; it was as simple as that. People took the law into their own hands as needed. Sometimes it worked; sometimes it didn't. But the Mexican way seemed to say—try it and see if it will fly.

We found ourselves thrown into a situation that was out of our hands—not for the first time, and not for the last. We thanked Reynoldo, and left Merida for the coast.

⎯⎯➤◆◀⎯⎯

Back in Puerto Morelos we met with Joe Marino.

"Did Reynoldo have everything in order for you?" he asked.

I fielded the question, "Yes, we're all set with the paperwork, now we have to send papers to the owners, have them sign, and then we'll pay them. After that, Reynoldo will file everything for us. Maybe we should call them tonight and let them know we have things set up for our *fideicomiso.*"

"Good idea," Joe agreed. "Then you'll feel it's safe to continue with the project."

"Safe? What do you mean?" Paul asked.

"Talk to the owners, make sure everything is okay with them. They can be quirky; best to talk with them first. Use my phone and let's get this out of the way. You'll feel better," he instructed.

We walked into his cubbyhole of an office. The air conditioning was going full bore. His dog, an all white Samoyan named Houndie, was lying on a handsome, Mexican rug of rich, dark colors; if anyone or anything needed air conditioning, it was definitely Houndie, with all that fur. A Siamese cat named Sid brushed against my legs, looking for an affectionate pat. I acquiesced.

"Here's the number. Now, don't look so nervous; it's going to be fine," Joe assured Paul, handing him the phone.

Paul dialed the number and in seconds had the owner on the line.

"Hello, this is Paul Zappella calling, from Mexico. How are

you?" After exchanging pleasantries he said, "Yes, we're still here. We just got back from the notary's office and he's put together preliminary paperwork on the *fideicomiso* for us."

Then Paul's face contorted. "You're not sure about the deal? We were under the impression you'd made up your mind. Oh, you need some time?"

Joe and I exchanged looks. It suddenly became apparent why Reynoldo wanted us to cover our bases with the property owners.

"When should I call you back? Sure, I totally understand. It must be a devastating experience, losing your land like that." Paul was shaking his head and rolling his eyes skyward.

"Okay," he continued. "I'll talk to you tomorrow afternoon. Hmm, hmm. I understand," Paul said as he set down the phone and sunk into one of Joe's office chairs.

"What happened?" I asked.

"She's nervous about the whole thing. Now she said maybe they want to rebuild. Can you believe it?"

"What?" I cried, going over to Paul and squeezing in beside him on the chair. "Oh, honey, not again."

"They're unpredictable," said Joe, shaking his head. "She was positive about selling two days ago when I talked to her."

"Well, she needs time to think right now," said Paul, shrugging his shoulders. "What can we do? We just have to wait her out and see what happens tomorrow. Now I know why Reynoldo was so insistent about taking care of us." He now held my hand in a tight grip.

"What did Reynoldo do?" Joe asked.

"He insisted on putting in a clause that said the property was ours when she signed the papers, before money changes hands. We said it didn't sound right, but he insisted on it, and said he wasn't going to change it."

"We had no choice," I continued for Paul, as his hand tightened on mine. "Plus we'd run out of time."

"There's nothing to do now but wait. And with Reynoldo, he has good sense and he follows his feelings. He must have liked you to put the package together like that."

Paul sighed, "Here we go—the waiting game again."

"I am so disgusted with everything!"

"Just relax, don't worry," instructed Joe. "I don't think they want to keep the property. She's just going through her natural progression of should we, or shouldn't we? Paul, you played it well. You didn't get frustrated. That's good. I think she'll see things your way tomorrow."

"That put a damper on *our* night, when things were going so well," Paul responded.

"Don't worry," Joe insisted, ever the optimist. "Just remember Scarlett O'Hara's famous line, 'I'll think about it tomorrow.'"

"It feels great to be so totally in control of my life," I dead panned. "Why is everyone we deal with on Mexican land deals so bizarre? Is this a pre-requisite for Mexico?"

"Maybe it's just Mexico," Paul said. "Maybe Mexico *does* it to people. I think it's beginning to do it to me."

"Oh, Joe's right. Let's try not to worry about it. Tomorrow is another day, and maybe everything will work out. You said you'd talk to her tomorrow afternoon. Maybe we should discuss construction with Joe for now. Take our minds off the owners. Let's face it. It's not the worst thing that's happened to us on this topsy-turvy ride. Will we ever forget the eminent domain nightmare?"

Joe's eyebrows shot up as he gave me a quizzical look. I shrugged and began to tell him that chapter in our extensive history of land deals in Mexico.

Construction

Construction thoughts soon overshadowed the dilemna of the land crisis. After all, the owner had said yes to our offer twice. We were two-for-one on the shifting land deal. Either way, we knew there was still one more beachfront lot for sale in Puerto Morelos. Since the seller's decision was out of our hands, we opted to talk seriously with Joe Marino about construction.

We met Joe and his engineer, Enrique, early the next morning for a marathon meeting that covered countless topics, including placement of the footprint—or baseline—of the house, should things work out in our favor.

Due to the constant threat of hurricanes, we decided to set the house much farther back from the shoreline than Barry's house. In our estimation, both he and Alejandro had placed their homes far too close to the waterline, especially without seawalls to save them, should a hurricane strike.

Another thing we took into consideration was the public use law for all Mexican beaches. Mexico required that twenty meters from the high tide line be designated as federal land. In Mexico, beaches belong to everyone. We certainly didn't want to tamper with the feds, and aimed for ample setback in case erosion took over decades later.

After *Gilberto*'s lesson, we opted for a sea wall that would extend twelve feet above and twelve feet beneath the ground. We also planned to use the house debris as an additional barricade against hurricanes by crushing it to rubble and pushing it against the sea wall, in a similar effort to Rodolfo's use of his concrete terrace. We reminded ourselves, again, that most structural damage from hurricanes was caused by water surge rather than wind velocity.

Water surge would continue to pound away at a house foundation as long as a hurricane hovered over an area, and given enough time, it might eventually undermine it. With the rubble from Barry's house firmly planted between the twelve-foot seawall and the foundation, if a storm were to stall out over us, it would have to conquer this rubble first before eating the foundation. Presumably, this design would take the wrath of a water surge.

For all these reasons, we set our footprint much closer to the road than to the beach. In so doing, we discovered we could save part of Barry's old driveway. It had been constructed from whitewashed Mayan rock and would be a nice addition to the property.

That afternoon, we explained to Joe and the engineer, Enrique, how the house was formed in three movable sections, set in saw-tooth fashion, stretching ninety feet from bow to stern. The sprawling property size allowed for this.

The day's discussions focused on typical building matters: where to place doors and windows, ceiling height, bedroom size, bathroom placement, floor levels, kitchen size, curved walls, and the possibility of a second story some day. All in all, it was a productive day. After many hours we called it quits, and went back to Joe's to call the owner.

Luck was with us: she finally decided to sell. She assured Paul this was her final decision.

Another celebration was in order. When in Mexico, any reason at all was cause to celebrate. We decided to continue our house construction conversation over dinner, so we all piled into Joe's car and headed into town to a local restaurant. Frozen margaritas seemed a worthy celebratory drink, a perfect fit for a Mexico land deal.

We made plans to send off the *fideicomiso* first thing when we got back to the States, and once the seller received it, we would discuss the payoff.

————————

Back in San Francisco a few days later, we heard from the owner. Again, our hearts did a mad tango as we waited to decipher her mood du jour, but she was still firm on the deal. She decided to send her sister to San Francisco to handle the transaction. The sister would bring the documents and we'd give her a cashier's check in return.

So, the land was unceremoniously transferred into our names a few days later, our bank account was noticeably lighter, and we were proud owners of land in Puerto Morelos, Quintana Roo, Mexico.

When we had last been in Mexico, we set up a contractor's schedule with Joe and the engineer dividing overall costs into a twelve-month timeline. After an initial deposit for the immediate purchase of building materials, we decided to begin construction in January, 1991. Joe told us the house would be finished by Christmas. It sounded too good to be true. The budget and timing were set. We sent off our first payment and waited for the shock to set in. It was really happening . . . .

————————

Paul left for Mexico mid-January to help lay out the footprint and make sure everything was positioned properly on the lot. The day he arrived coincided with the beginning of the first Gulf War in Iraq. He took a late night flight and arrived early January

20. His first stop was *Posada Amor* for breakfast. Mexico City TV newscasters had just announced a red alert. According to Mexico TV, Saddam Hussein had shot a biological warfare missile at Israel.

Paul was in the middle of a Mexico meltdown. Everyone went crazy in the restaurant, and he had no idea why. His Spanish was poor, and everyone was so upset, he could barely make contact with a soul. He finally corralled someone into telling him what the news report said. Then he understood.

It wasn't until a day later that Mexico news stations retracted their statement, explaining Iraq had not used biological warfare. So much for the reliability of Mexican news. This would foreshadow things to come. Eight years later, the same Mexican TV station would broadcast that Hurricane Mitch, another horrendous class-five hurricane, had wiped out large portions of Central America and devastated Cancun.

Although Mitch's initial path was destined for Cancun, it stalled out over Honduras for five days, causing tremendous destruction before heading northward. Honduras' president said it would take that country thirty-five years to recover from the wreckage. By the time it came within range of Cancun, it had lost steam, and was no longer a real threat to the city. Cancun had been saved; Honduras had been sacrificed.

But no one would ever know it by watching Mexico City TV news. Ten-year old photos of Cancun after 1988's Hurricane *Gilberto* were continuously splashed across the screen, showing heavy storm damage with reports that Cancun was incapacitated and unable to accommodate tourists for the coming high season due to the hurricane. Since Cancun had been declared the original strike zone, viewers believed the onscreen photos were current.

This blatant deception was broadcast for two days before being rectified. When family or friends called from the States to see if we were okay, we explained we were fine; the storm had missed us. We had some high winds, but nothing bad.

Why was false news being broadcast? A reliable source explained that Mexico City TV stations owned innumerable hotel properties in Acapulco. By showing 1988 footage of hurricane damage to Cancun on worldwide TV, they hoped to convince nervous tourists to abandon their Cancun travel plans and re-book in safe, sunny Acapulco for Christmas.

Acapulco had fallen out of favor with tourists over the past several years, having grown too fast due to lack of city planning. Broadcasting false advertising would boost Acapulco's bookings for high season, and topple Cancun's popularity, at least temporarily. This put a whole new spin on the reliability of Mexico's news services . . . in Mexico, money didn't talk, it shouted.

For Paul, the next week went quickly. He watched the contractors and workers measure the dimensions for the footprint and mark it with limestone, then set boundaries with strings. Hard to imagine an entire house would be laid out without a level, but this was the Mayan way. A string was tied to a steel plumb bob, and each brick would be set and checked, straight as an arrow.

Joe Marino had assembled a work crew, five Mayans, who were now entrusted with the job of building our Mexican dream house. Ramon, the foreman, was in his thirties. Three other workers, Alberto, Simon and Ricardo, all mid-twenties, labored under him. The youngest on the crew was Felipe, sixteen at best, who was the go-fer and apprentice. He took on the most taxing jobs: cement mixing, hauling, all things the others weren't expected to do. But they had all occupied his position at one time. That was how an *albañil,* or stoneworker, learned the trade, through apprenticeship.

The Mayans' first task was to build themselves a shed out of tar paper, where they would live while constructing the house. As most workers came from *pueblos* sometimes hours away by bus, this would allow them to live cheaply while they worked.

Common practice among Mayan workers was a full month of work, six days a week, from dawn to dusk; then they would take a long weekend with their family back in their *pueblo*. This was a throwback to earlier times, no doubt. For centuries, Mayan men tended their maize fields during planting times, and could be gone forty days or more at a time. The maize fields were a long distance from the *cocal*, or "plantation." A *cocal* consisted of two or three *palapas* and a random grove of coco palms, usually occupied by one family. While the men were absent, the women cared for home and hearth. To this day, this custom is common in the Yucatan.

Workers living on a project site provided security both day and night, a necessity, as materials could be dropped off sometimes months in advance. If a rumor surfaced on possible cost increases, contractors ordered ahead of time and held materials at the site to save on the budget.

Our initial down payment had purchased building materials. Pick-up trucks came and went, depositing loads of cement blocks, and bags, or *bolsas*, of dry cement. Dump trucks filled with sand, gravel, and the ever-present *sascab* also made deliveries. But before these materials would be used, the first item on the agenda was bringing in a bulldozer to demolish what was left of Barry's old house.

After Joe Marino found a reliable source, bulldozing the remains of the ruined house only took a few days, since not much rebar had been used in the old house. That done, all the debris would be crushed down and pushed against the new sea wall. To create the sea wall, workers took two wood boards and lined them up, goal post style on one end, and drew a string to the other end where another batter board was set up, like two long parallel clothes lines. Rocks were then piled one on top of the other for the entire height of the frame, and fresh cement was poured in to solidify it all together.

No rocks ever extended outside the imaginary line set up by the string. After the cement hardened, now in sea wall form, the house debris would be pushed against it, directly in front of the house foundation. This, too, would serve as protection against future storms.

Eventually, we would add topsoil to this area and seed a lawn, but for the time being, it was an unattractive pile of rubble. The house would be set behind this, farther back from the water's edge, out of reach of a sea in turmoil.

Next on the agenda was house foundation. Joe Marino planned to make what he called a "wedding cake" foundation. By creating a lip approximately ten percent larger around than the house footprint, this bottom-heavy base would act as protection to any surge, should the house ever take a direct hit from a hurricane.

Like the sea wall, building the foundation was a massive project. The workers began by digging down to near water level. First, they created a layer of concrete which was mixed by hand, one bag of cement at a time. This portion of the foundation would grow to six feet in height, bringing its total height to seven feet or more before a final concrete layer was poured for the perimeter foundation. Then cement building blocks would sit on top of this final layer produced by the blood, sweat, and tears of the five Maya workers. And for their labors, they would receive Mexico's going rate in 1991 for construction workers—between thirty and fifty pesos a day, depending on each man's ability. This came to $3 to $5 U.S. dollars. Laying the foundation took five weeks.

I suppose we should have had nagging concerns about starting this venture—having a 2,500 square foot house built in a foreign country where the peso was fluctuating madly and we weren't fluent in the language. But oddly, we had none. Maybe after six years of playing the waiting game for our dream house, we were simply anesthetized. Maybe we had "gone loco," or maybe it was just time to begin. I had no qualms about the project, and had total confidence in our contractor, engineer and builders.

Our city friends never failed to ask, "Aren't you nervous about building a house in Mexico?"

We would truthfully respond, "Not at all; we're sleeping like babies." And we, finally, were.

Local Color

Paul's initial visit to the site went quickly and he returned to San Francisco full of stories and hope. All we had to do to hold up our end of the bargain was keep sending money. It seemed a simple task. Joe Marino had the hard part. He had to build a designer-style house in the outback Mayan jungle, using unsophisticated tools. But when Paul and I discussed the building process, we kept returning to a simple fact: the Mayans had built the pyramids. Innumerable monuments still stood from their heady days as rulers of the Americas, one thousand years after being created, as evidenced by Chichen Itza, Uxmal, Palenque, Tikal. Why tear apart a foolproof process?

As California's seasonal rains subsided and winter moved towards spring, we planned another Mexican vacation to coincide with Easter. Since house construction had been underway for three months, we would be able to see progress and discuss interior design details with Joe.

We arrived at the Cancun Airport in high spirits a few days before the holiday. We rented a car and headed straight to Joe Marino's, where we'd be staying in one of his *cabañas*. We rang the bell at his villa and Juan Jose, his caretaker, ushered us in from the sweltering heat of the street to the cool solitude of the garage and adjoining pool and terrace.

"*Hola*," Joe greeted us as he came from the main house. "How was your trip? Let's sit down and catch up." Joe waved us towards deck chairs near the swimming pool. The water looked refreshingly cool, a sharp contrast to the Yucatan heat.

As we settled into comfortable, padded chairs, Joe took a seat next to us. The thick, Mexican tiled terrace, reflecting the sunlight, felt warm beneath my now bare feet. A lazy wood bee examined the sienna-colored trumpet vine that clung steadfastly to one of the *cabañas* nearby.

"We're on schedule," he reported, "and the crew is working well. We have the walls up on the house, but you've seen that from the last photos I sent you."

We nodded our heads in unison. Paul's knee touched mine under the table and we shared a smile. "We've finished placing the windows and now we're getting ready to pour the roof. In order to ensure a uniform pour, we've decided to hire a cement company and truck to mix it."

This was uncommon in Mexico as all cement was usually mixed by hand.

"The roof is so large, we want to make sure all the cement is mixed at the same consistency so the roof sets properly. In Mexico, most roofs are smaller than yours, so the crew mixes cement bag by bag, but with that, you can't always predict the quality of the pour. Using a cement mixer will ensure not getting a cold pour, which occurs when part of the cement is already set and fresh cement is added. With a roof this size, that could happen. The mixer assures a uniform pour.

"After the roof is completed, it's a tradition for the contractor to buy the crew a case of beer. Pouring the roof is the hardest part of the entire building process, and the beer is their compensation for their aching bones," he finished.

Our timing allowed us to see just what pouring the roof entailed. The work crew assembled and the youngster on the team, Felipe, was literally low man on the totem pole. He went back and forth from the cement truck carrying five gallon buckets of cement. As he approached the hand-made *zapote* ladder, fashioned from branches lashed together with rope, Felipe lifted the cement-filled bucket onto his head. He balanced the bucket, grabbed the ladder with his other hand, and ascended to the roof. The process was so strenuous, he could have been a trained Olympic athlete rather than a construction worker.

On the roof, the other workers poured out the bucket of cement, then smoothed the gritty liquid into place in long, sweeping motions with a mop-like apparatus. While watching this methodical, tiring process, I questioned the American myth regarding Mexican work ethics.

We knew these men worked long hours, six days a week, struggling to build our house. The only difference in their work schedule versus an American work schedule was that in Mexico, the hour-long mid-day break was scheduled for the hottest part of the day—a time to eat tortillas and vegetables, and no matter where they were, time for the famous siesta. Workers could sleep on grass, rocks, sidewalks, under trees—anywhere. I think Americans misinterpreted the siesta break, and created a stereotype about this hardworking culture that was unfounded.

Over the years, we observed workers walking to work as few had bicycles, and their work day started at 6 or 7 a.m., which meant they had to wake up at 5 a.m. to start a day that lasted until dark. In a country with ninety-six million people, and only one percent of the population over age sixty-two, I knew they weren't dying from boredom. These people were hard workers.

Joe Marino told us that the independent *albañil* enlisted his sons into service early on so someone in the family could continue with the back-breaking work his profession required, before the father's consitution gave out at age forty. One rarely saw a man over that age in this trade, he assured us. The work was too vexing.

That night we'd been invited to a party thrown by an

American couple, Alan and Joan, who sold satellite TV systems for commercial and residential properties. They had a number of large hotels as clients in the hotel zone.

As we walked to the party from Joe's house, he gave us a run-down on the characters in the Puerto Morelos social scene.

"There's quite a cast assembled here," he warned us. "Don't be surprised if the party gets rowdy."

We were just a few blocks away. The evening sky was in dusk mode, a few stars making an early appearance. Springtime was my favorite season in Mexico. Tropical flowers grew everywhere, in every color imaginable.

Party sounds filled the night air along with the scent of night-blooming jasmine. As we approached, even in the twilight (Puerto Morelos had no street lights at that time), I noticed a similarity to all the houses on the block. All were shaped like square boxes, the only variation being color. They were cement block in structure. Not much imagination had been used in design. We later nicknamed this strip of homes Gringo Row.

On arriving at Alan and Joan's and entering, Joe yelled, "Duck!"

He wasn't kidding, and just in time. Given normal height, anyone entering would hit his or her head on the low door entry.

"Thanks for the warning," Paul said.

"That's nothing. Wait until you have to use the john," Joe replied mysteriously.

"What does that mean?" I asked.

"Don't worry, you'll see. But I'll just give you one word of warning."

"Duck?" I guessed.

"Definitely, and be glad you took some time with your design details."

"I'm glad already," I mumbled. "Look at this place. *No* design and it's dark as a cave."

Although the house was nicely furnished in a rustic motif—attractive wall hangings made from hand-dyed wool in dark, exotic colors, leather furniture from central Mexico, intricate, carved frames on elegant paintings—the shape and the design of the living room was far from ideal. The windows were small and made from the cheapest aluminum; the wall finish appeared to be at least a half inch thick, as though cement had literally been thrown on the wall, with no attempt at smoothing it out at all. I knew this finish style was popular in Mexico, but it simply didn't appeal to me. Let's just say the house had a lot of "don'ts." It wouldn't win any Architectural Digest awards.

"Come this way and I'll introduce you to the hosts," Joe said as he steered me by the arm towards the kitchen, another architectural glitch. It was windowless and the ceiling was barely seven feet high. Maybe this *was* a cave. Thank goodness a door opened onto a backyard patio, for fresh air and light. Cooking here would be far from pleasurable.

"Alan and Joan, I'd like you to meet Paul and Jeanine. I'm building a house for them north of town; where Barry's old house was."

"Nice to meet you," Alan said, with a smile that bordered on a grimace. He was in his late forties, had a receding hairline and a slick appearance. A bit too polished for old Mexico, I thought. Joan extended her hand, then smiled. She had ducktail short brunette hair and doe-like brown eyes. She was wearing jeans and an embroidered Mayan blouse, peasant style.

"Nice to meet you, too," Paul replied.

"Looks like a great party," I offered, as I watched the room start to fill with people, almost before my eyes. I guess we'd arrived at the bewitching hour.

"Oh, the fun has just begun," Joan replied with a smile. "How about a couple of beers?"

"Fine."

Joan excused herself, heading towards the kitchen in search of drinks. I struck up a conversation with Alan, curious about the local gringos who would soon be our neighbors. He was wearing tight black jeans and a black stretch tee-shirt that would have looked good on someone half his age with twice his physique.

"Have you been in Puerto Morelos long?" I asked.

"Just a year. We lived in Cancun until a year ago, then decided to move farther down the coast and found Puerto Morelos."

"Where are you from?" I asked.

"Los Angeles," his reply. "I was CEO for a software company that I started. After a few years, the stress got to me so I sold, and got the hell out. Decided it was time to bail, leave L.A. and the smog."

"Did you sell your home?" I asked, curious about anyone who had ditched the States and moved south to Mexico. I wondered how others afforded the move, how they'd adjusted. Also, being from California, I knew any conversation about real estate was an icebreaker. No one could could believe the inflation; and this was the '80s. More unbelievable yet was that buyers were paying those prices, and they just kept escalating.

"Oh, we didn't own a home there. We just didn't want the responsibility," he answered.

"Well, probably good to get out of the rat race," I answered, but an alert went off in my head. Something didn't compute. Here was a former CEO of a software company and he didn't own a home? Having worked in Silicon Valley for the past several years, I knew the rich rewards of the tech industry, and the reputations of these CEOs. They certainly weren't shy about owning property, and oftentimes their home acquisitions were fodder for the local media. The '80s were the heady days of

Apple, Intel, Hewlett-Packard, and Motorola. Then I remembered Joe told me Alan and Joan were renting this house, too. Hmmm. Something was amiss.

"We love Mexico," Alan was saying as I caught myself zooming back to the conversation. "We started a satellite TV business here. We've been putting in satellites for hotels in the hotel zone, plus we also install residential services. If you're ever in the market for satellite, let me know."

"We're just building now, but thanks for the offer. I'm not sure if we'll have a TV, but it's good to know we can contact you if we decide to have one."

It wouldn't be until a year later that my suspicions about Alan and Joan were confirmed. We had just arrived in Mexico for Christmas and before going to the house, took a drive around the town square to see what, if anything, was going on.

A Christmas committee had hung a string or two of Christmas lights around the concrete gazebo in the center of the *zócalo*. Paul pointed out they had tapped directly into the electrical pole for their electric usage, stealing power to run their holiday lights. Christmas time—the gift of giving, or something like that. We were laughing about it, commenting on how long it would take to be discovered in California before PG&E figured out the ruse, when we noticed a lone figure walking around the town square.

"Who's that?" I asked Paul.

"I'm not sure," he replied. "Wait a minute; I think it's Joan."

"Let's see what's up. Pull over."

Paul stopped the rental car and called out the window to the shadowy form of a woman. She turned her head and stared at us as we called her name; then she recognized us and began walking our way.

"When did you get in?" she said, with a slight sniffle.

"Just now. So what's happening?" Paul asked.

"Oh, I'm just looking for Alan," she answered, her voice cracking.

"Looking for Alan?" I asked, mystified, wondering how anyone could get lost in Puerto Morelos.

"Yes, he's disappeared. About three days ago. I thought he might be back, so I decided to look for him on the square," she explained, while she pulled a tissue from her pocket and quietly blew her nose. I wondered if she was going to turn up rocks, look behind trees.

Paul and I exchanged looks. "So, you don't know where he is?"

"No, he's gone," she moaned. "I don't know what happened. We'd planned a big New Year's Day party. But even if he's not back, I'm having the party. You'll come, won't you? I already bought a ham and I'm making it with brine. You can't find cured hams in Mexico." For a moment her manner changed dramatically, as if preparation for this party could make up for a missing spouse. I wondered about her sanity—not for the first time.

"Sure, we'll come," I answered as Paul flashed me an evil look. "I hope Alan shows up."

"Not half as much as I do," Joan said with heavy sarcasm, seeming now to have forgotten her party menu.

As soon as we were mobile again, I said to Paul, "We had to accept that invitation. My God, what could I say?"

"I don't want to go. Is there any way to get out of it?"

We learned later from Joe Marino that Alan had skipped town a few days before, right after collecting for dozens of satellite units that were supposed to be hooked up before the holidays, when all the Bowl games were happening. The satellites, sadly, were never installed. Why was I not surprised?

He and his spicy, little secretary, Conchita, left Mexico for Florida to start life anew in the Sunshine State, leaving Joan behind, or so went the rumor. I wondered if satellite would be in Alan's future.

We were beginning to understand old Mexico by this time. It was way different from the U.S.

"It seems like a weird thing to do for someone who owned a software company. I told Joe. "Was he a man with a checkered past? What a strange guy."

"Did you say a software company?" Joe asked.

"Yes, he told me he started a software company. But moving to Mexico, then running away with the secretary? It just doesn't match the M.O. of a CEO."

"Is that what he told you? He said he owned a software company?" Joe chortled. "Oh man! The guy produced underground films in L.A."

"You're kidding!"

"Afraid not!" Joe said.

"So he's gone with the cash, and won't be honoring those satellite contracts?"

"You can bet on it. Let's just say a lot of people who were expecting to watch the silver ball drop at Times Square for New Year's won't be watching it via satellite . . . not in Puerto Morelos, anyway."

"Is this my first social science lesson in Mexico? Watch out for expatriates and forget satellite?"

"Actually, you have to watch people wherever you go. But in Mexico, that's why we build such big walls. To avoid contact as much as possible. Are you sure you don't want me to give you a quote for a wall, all the way around your property?" he pressed.

"No," I insisted. "You know we don't want a wall. I don't think we need one, besides, I like the people here in Mexico."

"Sure, but mark my words. Some day, you will have three things: a wall, a TV—maybe not with satellite—and air conditioning."

"No way!" I protested.

On New Year's Day we dropped by Joan's house for her fiesta. It was definitely lacking sizzle. Alan hadn't surfaced, naturally, and she'd had a whole week to adjust to her new lifestyle which consisted of selling everything she owned. When we arrived for her party, the house was stripped bare; it hardly looked like the same house we'd been to a couple years earlier. Getting to know fellow gringos was already proving to be an unusual experience. I'd never met people quite like this in the U.S.

"Happy New Year's? Or, whatever," I mumbled, as Joan opened the front door. I ducked and entered, and Paul followed.

"Thanks. I've definitely had better."

I glanced around the now barren house. A Hoover couldn't have sucked up every trace of her belongings any better, except for a lone Christmas tree, complete with decorations, taking center stage in the living room. There was an awkward silence as I heard the hissing of a pot on the stove in the kitchen, no doubt cooking the prized ham. At least she wouldn't starve to death. Not tonight, anyway.

"Nice tree," I said, breaking the silence.

"Do you want to buy it?" She was serious.

"No, thanks anyway," I murmured as Paul and I exchanged looks.

We hung around for twenty minutes before I invented a handy excuse—we were late for another party.

———

Joan's party did pick up speed that earlier night, our first foray into the Puerto Morelos social scene, while we were building the house. People danced, music blared, tequila flowed. Then around 11 p.m. the electricity flickered and in moments, a blackout. No one seemed surprised and candles emerged from cupboards as if on cue. Staples of life in Mexico—flashlight, candles, matches. The party didn't miss a beat.

This was our first encounter with the expatriates—they were festive, restless, and rowdy. But we weren't immune to the party atmosphere and figured we were along for the ride. *Bienvenidos.* Welcome to Mexico.

So Far From God

That Easter week was a montage of meetings at the work site and late night discussions with Joe Marino about the direction we would take on the interior design of the house. We pulled up to Joe's house late one afternoon after a serious shopping trip in Cancun.

The dusty street was empty except for a battered white pick-up truck parked by his garage. Inside the truck, a round-faced man with jet black hair was reviewing a sheaf of papers. He looked up, and when he saw us, he flashed a wide smile. I smiled back. He was nimbly out of the truck before we turned off the motor and parked at the curb. Wearing jeans and a Forty-Niners' tee shirt that just covered his ample, upper body, he moved with uncharacteristic grace for a man his size. In a second he was standing by our car door.

"*Hola*," he said, the universal Mexico greeting. "*Soy* Arturo."

"Arturo? Do you work with wood?" I asked, practicing my Spanish.

"*Si, si*," he responded, pleased that I recognized him to be the carpenter whose skill approached artistry.

I had been admiring his mahogany windows, doors and closets in Joe Marino's house for the past six months, and it seemed I was always asking who produced the incredible woodwork.

"And who are you?" he asked in Spanish.

"Juanita *y* Pablo," I replied. For years during our travels in

Mexico, we'd always gone by the Spanish equivalent of our names. In our early travel days, it just seemed appropriate.

"*Seguro!*" Arturo responded. Of course. Then he excitedly shook our hands in rapid succession. Immediately he rattled off a long paragraph in Spanish, and at that moment I promised myself I would learn the language. I would sign up for yet another Spanish class at a community college when we returned to California. I wanted to communicate in my soon-to-be-adopted country. To my surprise, I was the exception rather than the rule. Among my acquaintances, I counted only a handful of gringos who spoke flawless Spanish. Odd, when considering the insistence Americans placed on the need for perfect English from any foreigner arriving on U.S. shores. Mexicans, on the other hand, gave wide berth to foreigners lacking Spanish language skills.

Even though my Spanish was limited, I decided to practice what I knew with Arturo. I put aside my shyness and attempted to tell him why we were in Mexico—to check the status of the house construction—and how pleased we were with the results. By the time Joe arrived, we were old friends.

"I see you've met Arturo," Joe said as he got out of his car. "We've known him for years. He first began working with my father, while he was still living full time in Merida, and now he works with me. What began as a one-man show has blossomed into a twelve-man crew, and they're all related."

"Great," I said, nodding my approval.

I noticed Arturo was trying to follow Joe's conversation. "*Hablas inglés?*" I asked.

He responded that he was trying to learn English as I was attempting Spanish. At that point Joe intervened, and suggested Arturo and I work on our language skills together. We were both at the same entry level, and he assured me it was an effective learning method.

I quickly agreed and as the years progressed and my Spanish improved, I found Arturo not only a prize language instructor, but also an apt tutor of Yucatan history.

First, though, he told us how he'd become a woodman, or *maestro de madera*, in Puerto Morelos, after having worked in management for twelve years at a large Mexican bank in Merida, the banking capital of the Yucatan.

Arturo had worked as a loan administrator, and at the time there was a lot of graft going to various bank employees in exchange for favors granted. Others in his department had put loans on hold for weeks, even months, feigning too much work. But actually, he explained, they were just shiftless.

Sometimes this delay would work in the bank employee's favor, however. If a loan package lingered too long without approval, some clients would come up with a gift, *regalo,* to entice the loan officer to finalize the paperwork.

In one instance, Arturo recalled his entire department accepted gifts of one thousand hectares of land in exchange for completing illegal paperwork. This particular client pursued Arturo's acceptance of the plan relentlessly, but Arturo refused to be included. He explained to us he knew illegal proceedings were taking place, but by doing his work and looking the other way, he hoped to avoid any connection to the fraud. He needed a job; he was stuck.

Six months later, *federales* stormed into the loan department offices. Everyone was arrested that day except Arturo. He resigned later that week, deciding he'd rather be unemployed than incarcerated.

In Mexico, he explained, governors became very rich by calling in favors owed to them. Oftentimes their compensation came through prime real estate holdings. So as not to be obvious about the amount of land they owned, they would use people who were referred to as *presta nombres*. *Presta nombres* would sign the land titles on these called-in favors, using their name rather than the governor's, so the governor did not attract scrutiny by showing up as title holder on too many pieces of property, all acquired during his term in office.

Their reward for signing usually came through land acquisitions or cash. So the *presta nombres* got rich along with the governor. According to Arturo, governors in all Mexican states became wealthy on illegal land dealings. Mario Villanueva, governor of Quintana Roo until 1999, was a perfect example.

His notoriety came from selling off one thousand hectares of federal land in the Riviera Maya south of Cancun—prime beachfront, no less—to Spanish hotel chains for the construction of all-inclusive resorts. For his final coup in office, he attempted to sell off land at Xcacel, near Tankah, one of the last known sanctuaries for green and loggerhead sea turtles. Fortunately, this fraudulent sale was put on temporary hold in 2001, when environmentalists sued the company's plans for a thousand-room hotel next to the spot where the turtles bred and laid eggs in the summer, according to a New York Times article.

But Villanueva's corruption didn't stop at nefarious land dealings. He was indicted in a New York federal court for helping to smuggle two hundred tons of Columbian cocaine into the U.S. from Mexico, with his fee at $500,000 per shipment. Villanueva was arrested in Cancun in May, 2001. He had been on the run since disappearing from Cancun nine days before his term as governor ended in August, 1999. During Villanueva's reign, a mysterious luxury yacht showed up near the Palancar Reef in Puerto Morelos one morning in January 1999. When the Mexican Navy went to investigate, they found the seventy foot craft floating along empty, no one on board. They also found sixty empty barrels—thirty white, thirty blue. Puerto Morelos is thirty hours from Columbia, and the white barrels filled with diesel would have been just enough fuel to transport the million dollar vessel to our port town; the blue barrels contained cocaine, we were told. Apparently smuggling cocaine was lucrative enough that million dollar yachts could be scrapped as part of the cost of doing business. We were told a handoff most likely took place at night, and the cocaine was probably transferred to a less conspicuous vessel. The yacht disappeared a few days later. No one in our port authority knew where it went, but that winter everyone in town ended up with a blue garbage can, salvaged off the mystery ship.

Former Mexican presidents have docked in as some of the wealthiest men in the world. Carlos Salinas' example still stands as proof that political leanings pay big in Mexico. In his case, his entire family profited. However, at present, his brother Raul is still detained in a Mexico City prison due to his involvement in drug and money laundering cases which occurred during his brother's presidential tenure.

Raul Salinas was also implicated in two political murders, but was never brought to trial on those counts, as no evidence could be obtained to directly link him to the crimes, a friend told us. But, our friend said, at least some justice was served; Raul still sits in prison and is paying the price for abuse of power. Meanwhile, ex-president Carlos resides far from the hand of justice in Ireland, a country that refuses extradition to Mexico.

After the *federales* stormed the bank's offices and Artruro left their employ in need of work, he found a job as a house painter in Merida for a contractor named Estafen. At the time, Estafen was working for Joe's dad in Puerto Morelos. Mr. Marino, Joe Senior, asked Arturo if he could paint houses, and Arturo assured him he could. After a few successful jobs, Mr. Marino asked if he could manufacture ten hardwood doors, explaining he desperately needed the doors within forty-eight hours, as another contractor had failed him. Arturo assured the older man he was as good as his word.

Two days later, the doors were finished. Mr. Marino was surprised his deadline had been met, and insisted on seeing Arturo's workshop. At the shop, he was shocked to find only basic carpentry tools, nothing electrical in the bunch. Arturo had met the schedule by hand manufacturing the hardwood doors in record time.

"How can you work like this?" Mr. Marino asked him. "Listen, I'll buy you the electrical equipment you need; then we'll see what you can do."

With this initiation, Arturo and Mr. Marino began a longtime friendship.

Arturo's personal history often gave us insight into the country we were adopting, and his anecdotes mirrored the workings of a society. Over time, more stories would be told, but in that first meeting, we'd established a camaraderie and friendship of our own.

Tales from the Yucatan

During 1991 Paul and I lived between two worlds, the world we knew well—corporate San Francisco, and the Yucatan, a mysterious place with an indigenous people called Maya in a jungle land bordered by a turquiose sea.

No doubt about it, we much preferred this latter place, for it represented freedom and a new life unfettered by stress and the pressures of our modern-day world. I believe if anyone is plotting out this type of endeavor, be it retirement or an extended adventure vacation, the best time is in the planning and preparation. As the adage goes, "It's not the destination, it's the journey."

One weekend while driving down the coast to Monterey, we stopped at Moss Landing, known only for its working boat harbor and a handful of antique shops. Tucked away next to an old railroad caboose turned antique shop was a used bookstore, Yesterday's Books. Intrigued, we peeked inside. A pencil-thin woman behind the antique cash register smiled at us. Apparently the owner, she lowered her no-frills glasses as we crossed the threshold, giving us a closer look. We passed inspection and she replaced the lenses firmly on her narrow nose, resuming her absorption in the sheaf of papers in front of her. The floor boards creaked, weary with age. A gray Persian cat stretched, moved towards us from its resting spot on a well-worn rug, and brushed my leg.

I stared idly at the rough, clapboard walls and the no-nonsense, unvarnished shelves holding up countless books. Her storefront had originally been a fish processing plant, detailing all aspects of production for canning sardines. Now it teamed with books, crammed in as tightly as the former residents. I slowly made my way to a rear corner of the shop where a faded sign marked "Mexico and Central America" hung crookedly over three shelves bulging with dusty volumes of travel books. Paul browsed in the nautical and boating section, one of his longtime passions, having owned a sailboat several years earlier.

I kneeled down, ready to rummage. A few of the more bizarre titles, like *I Married Adventure*, done up in a zebra-patterened hardcover, jumped out at me. Then, in my organized shuffling, I happened onto *The Lost World of Quintana Roo*, by Michel Peissel. Feeling excited, I anxiously turned to the inside dust flap, and fell under the spell of a world gone by.

"This is the true story of a remarkable adventure," it began. "Michel Peissel, a young Frenchman with an international background was stranded on the coast of Quintana Roo, in eastern Yucatan, abandoned by boatmen he had engaged to take him southward."

Peissel's tale was a tall adventure indeed, I was later to find out after devouring the book in just two sittings. He walked on foot from where the town of Puerto Morelos would eventually be located to Belize in 1958. After being abandoned by Mayan boatmen mere hours after a harrowing crossing from Cozumel, Peissel was just young and inexperienced enough at twenty-one to start out on foot wearing only sandals for a two hundred mile journey through dense jungles and mangrove swamps.

In 1958, there was absolutely nothing there—no roads, no houses, no form of civilization whatsoever. Rumor had it that this was where a young Fidel Castro came to train his band of guerillas before the Cuban uprising against Fulgencio Bautista in 1959, meaning the Quintana Roo Coast was then that desolate and remote.

Peissel found only a handful of coconut plantations called *cocals*, consisting of a single family and one or two grass hut *palapas*. After being abandoned, his only hope to exit the jungle was to travel from *cocal* to *cocal*, relying on the assistance of the Mayans who lived there for food, water and direction.

His adventure included being chased by *chiclero* bandits and encountering Chan Santa Cruz Indians, who until then killed any white man on sight as the Caste War of the Yucatan had just ended twenty years earlier. He partook in religious ceremonies with indigenous Mayans and stumbled onto undiscovered pyramid sites.

A voice behind me asked, "What did you find in the Mexcio section?"

I turned around and faced the owner. The Persian cat purred contentedly, cradled in the nook of her arm, as she peered down at the books I'd scattered onto the bleached wooden floor boards.

I held up the faded volume and answered, *"The Lost World of Quintana Roo.* Quite an epic."

"Oh, yes. That's a treasure all right. Intrepid—that's the only word for that young man! Walking on foot through Mexican jungles. My word."

"I guess you've read it then," I said, a little surprised she was familiar with the book.

"Oh, dear, of course. Mexico, the Aztec and the Maya . . . my special interest areas. When I was young, my parents took me on a trip to Mexico. We visited the pyramids at Teotihuacan, just north of Mexico City. I saw the Pyramid of the Sun and the Pyramid of the Moon. Made quite an impression on me, so I've studied the Aztec and the Maya my entire life. I read anything I can find on those subjects along with archeology, and when I'm finished with my reading, I put it here," she said, pointing to the overstuffed shelves in front of me.

"We're building a house in the Yucatan and now I'm fascinated by the Maya," I said. "Looks like I've come to the right spot."

"For background, you should read *The Plumed Serpent*, by D.H. Lawrence," the owner advised. "I'd also suggest *The Power and the Glory*, by Graham Greene. My name is Mildred, by the way. Goodness, what an adventure, building a house in Mexico."

"It has become one, that's for sure. I'm Jeanine, and that's Paul over there in your nautical section. What a great bookstore this is. How long have you had it?"

"Oh, dear," Mildred sighed, trying to recall dates and times. Apparently years had slipped by while she hunkered down in the time warp of this wood frame bookstore, seemingly unaware another world existed. She was cozy and warm in a shop on the Monterey Coast with her cat, her wood stove, and words from countless authors in thousands of books to keep her company.

"Let me see now. I guess I've had the store for almost sixteen years. I bought it with my pension money right after I retired. I was a high school librarian and I guess it kind of slipped over into my own life, didn't it?" she said thoughtfully, as if she just became aware of it.

"It's a great store. I have dreams of opening a bookstore, but in Mexico. How did you get started?" I asked as I followed her back up to the counter at the front of the store.

"Well, I was lucky. I found an estate sale where I bought my first eight thousand books. Then I started going to garage sales," she answered as she paused and picked up the copy of the *The Lost World of Quintana Roo* I was buying. Immediately her focus shifted, and she grabbed a pair of scissors to do a quick repair on the spine. In minutes it was flawless.

"Let me know how you like this book," Mildred said, "and *The Plumed Serpent,* and I'll jot down a few other titles on the Maya."

Paul called from the nautical section, "Jeanine, you have to see this ship. I think it pulled into the Puerto Morelos harbor."

"I'll be right back," I said to Mildred as I made my way down the aisle to the nautical and boating section where Paul was standing with an oversized title, *Sailing Ships of the 20th Century.* The book lay open to a magnificent photograph of the Fantome, a four-masted, three-hundred foot schooner.

"Listen to this," Paul instructed. "It says it was built for a duke in 1926, and later bought by Aristotle Onassis as a wedding gift for Princess Grace of Monaco. But the princess never invited Onassis to her wedding, so she never got the boat."

Indeed, the Fantome had sailed right into Puerto Morelos on several occasions as part of the Windjammer Barefoot Cruises Sailing Line. We were as shocked to see a ship of such magnitude in our little port town as were our neighbors.

Gazing at the book, I said, "The Windjammer Cruise ship. Yes. What a beauty."

Years later, this ship would come to an unseemly end. Caught in the throes of Hurricane Mitch, an unpredictable class five hurricane, the four-masted ship had been boxed in by the storm. After Mitch gained strength, becoming a major hurricane, thirty-two year old Guyan March, British Captain of the Fantome, was told by Windjammer President Michael Burke, Miami, to drop off paying passengers in Belize. The self-insured steel hull vessel had been refurbished in 1969 for an excessive amount, according to a 1998 *Miami Herald* article, and Captain March and thirty crew members were instructed to try and outrun the storm, heading at first northwards towards Cancun and the safety of the Gulf of

Mexico. But as the ship set sail, it became apparent that the hurricane had shifted direction, so Captain March turned the Fantome south, towards Honduras.

Mitch was now blowing at one hundred and eighty miles an hour and gaining strength. Just as Captain March headed north, the National Hurricane Center predicted Cancun would take the brunt of Mitch, as the storm shifted northwest towards the Yucatan Peninsula. The lumbering ship sailed only nine miles per hour, and would never outrun the storm. To further complicate matters, forecasters were having trouble predicting Mitch's path as the atmospheric currents were weak. Historically, hurricanes at that time of the season, late October, drifted north-northwest.

Then Mitch stopped. It stalled out in one location, never losing velocity. By this time, Captain March was left with two choices—either run south or east. Captain March headed south, towards the lee side of the island Roatan just off the Honduras coast. Then forecasters predicted yet another change in the storm—Mitch was dipping south and heading directly at Roatan. Now March's only choice was to again head north, or due east. He was being walled in by the storm. He chose east, hoping to slip into a safety slot as the eye passed above. When ship owner Burke last spoke to March, the Fantome was east of Roatan, Honduras, forty miles south of Mitch's eyewall. The captain told the owner he was battling one hundred mile-per-hour gale force winds and forty-foot waves, and he said Mitch was taking dead aim at him. Then all communication with the Fantome was lost.

Three days later, on Halloween, the ship, still missing, was nicknamed the Ghost Ship. Then on November 2, Mexico's Day of the Dead, after an intense three day search, eight life vests and two life rafts with the name SV/Fantome were found floating off the coast of Honduras. Some speculated that the steel hull ship may have pitch-poled, a stern-to-bow flip, with mast poles literally pitching forward and the bottom of the ship turning upside down which can happen when a ship encounters fifty-foot waves dead on. But no one will ever know the true account.

Mitch killed 10,000 people in Honduras and became the fifth most powerful Atlantic hurricane on record. In 1998, Cancun was saved, Honduras was sacrificed, along with the Ghost Ship, the Fantome.

But that day in Moss Landing, years earlier, we had no clue as to what fate had in store for the elegant four-masted schooner. What we did know was that Mildred's bookstore held certain fascination for both of us.

I handed the book back to Paul, and returned to the counter to collect my recent purchases.

"The next time you're in Moss Landing, drop in and we can chat about Mexico," Mildred said, pushing a slip of ivory paper my way. "I think you'll find these titles very interesting. They're a bit more scholarly."

"Thank you, Mildred," I said, clutching my new reading list. *"The Caste War of Yucatan,* by Nelson Reed, and *Maya Cosmos,* by Linda Schele and David Freidel. I can't wait to read them."

Thus began my search for literature on the Maya. Mildred continued to be a great source for us until we left for Mexico a couple years later. On rainy weekends we'd drive down the coast to Moss Landing to chat with Mildred about Mexico, the Maya, and her whimsical bookshop. These leisurely interludes were pleasant times and a welcome diversion as we labored our way through the dregs of our work-a-day world in the Bay Area, awaiting clemency.

Passionate Pilgrim

"Who was Alma Reed?" I asked Paul as we prepared dinner one Sunday evening in our home in Half Moon Bay. "Have you heard of her? I think she was born in San Francisco."

"She worked for the Hearst papers in the '20s. Covered the Fatty Arbuckle trial after the St. Francis Hotel incident. You know, the *first* trial of the century, before O.J? Arbuckle was falsely accused of murdering a woman at a wild party, with a Coke bottle, no less. It ruined his film career. I think she interviewed him."

"Did she have a connection to the Yucatan?"

"I know she was one of the first women news reporters in San Francisco," Paul said. "Either my mother or my grandmother told me that. Why?"

"I found this book at a garage sale, *Alma Reed, The Passionate Pilgrim* by Antoinette May. I started scanning the back cover and it mentioned Mexico and some romance with a governor. Sounds intriguing."

After finding this little known gem, I wanted to read all the books about Mexico and the Yucatan that had ever been written. Finding the Alma Reed book chronicling her tragic love story with Yucatan Governor Felipe Carrillo inspired me, but it was another book that actually led us to the Yucatan. I found an old copy of the two-volume set *Incidents of Travel in Central America, Chiapas and Yucatan*, (1841) and *Incidents of Travel In Yucatan* (1843) by John L. Stephens, with engravings by English artist Frederick

Catherwood. Stephens, a prominent New York attorney, was appointed U.S. diplomatic agent to Central America and asked by President Martin Van Buren to travel there on a confidential mission in 1839. Stephens planned to use this trip to extensively explore the Mayan ruins of Copan, Palenque, and Uxmal. Having met Catherwood on a trip to London, and well aware of the artists' famous drawings of digs at Egypt and Jerusalem, Stephens convinced him to join his upcoming expedition. The two set off for Central America and were the first English-speaking travelers to explore these regions originally settled by the Maya.

So popular was *Incidents of Travel* that it had twelve press runs its first year of publication. Adding to the mystery of these pyramids, along with Catherwood's incredible illustrations, was the fact that soon after Stephens and Catherwood returned to the U.S., the Caste War of the Yucatan began, virtually closing the Yucatan Peninsula for sixty years to anyone of white or light complexion. Only indigenous Maya could safely roam there; all Spanish and Mestizo were killed on sight. So Stephens' exploration was the only account available on the Maya pyramids throughout the 19th century, heightening the near hysteria for more information on the Maya and their palace-like structures overgrown with trees, deeply embedded in the Yucatan jungles. In Europe, *Incidents of Travel* sparked intense interest as various authorities on Atlantis, the lost continent, declared the Maya pyramids had been built by Atlantis' descendants. With Quintana Roo and Yucatan borders closed to explorers due to the Caste War, the Mayan pyramids were becoming the stuff of 19th century urban legend.

Catherwood's engravings were rendered with such skill that his drawings are still useful today. Although trained as an architect, his talent was in his capacity to draw ancient ruins with accuracy and insight. He developed a technique in drawing with the aid of a camera lucida, which was the precursor to the invention of modern photography. This assisted him in drawing in the dank, dark pyramids, where there was little exposure to sunlight. While Stephens toiled at excavating ruins, Catherwood worked while standing on top of crudely-made scaffolding, or sometimes in mud, covered in netting. He wore clumsy gloves to keep mosquitoes from attacking him while he drew. Both men continually suffered from malaria. Their bodies were ravaged and swollen from mosquito bites, yet they endured these intolerable conditions until Catherwood finally collapsed.

Stephens' account fascinated us, and Catherwood's drawings were strangely compelling. Shortly after reading *Incidents of Travel*, we made reservations for our first trip to the Yucatan. We had to see the Mayan pyramids. At that time, twenty years ago, the travel agent hadn't heard of Cancun nor the nearby island Isla Mujeres, and Paul had to convince her to get out a Mexico map so he could show her the location. A month later we were on a Mexicana flight, stopping only at the Cancun airport to catch a cab, then onto Isla Mujeres by boat, known only as the people's ferry.

We fell in love with Isla. Adored North Beach with the shallow, turquoise ocean bumping up onto a white sand beach that stretched seemingly for miles (standard fare for the Mexican Caribbean we were soon to find out) and especially loved Maria's, a small resort with French restaurant serving excellent cuisine. Maria had only five rooms to rent, bungalows fit for a tropical hideaway paradise, with *palapa* roofs, and a bountiful exterior garden brimming with hibiscus, crotons, and areca palms. A narrow cement walkway, etched with geckos and tropical flowers, wound its way down to the two prized bungalows, close enough to the beach to hear waves lapping on the shore at night. Although we'd started out in the less desirable rooms closer to the restaurant, we stayed long enough to nab one of the sought-after bungalows below. We spent long hours on Maria's lonesome beach, sharing the ocean with her ancient loggerhead sea turtles that swam in the ocean by day and by dusk returned to a funky *zapote* cage that straddled the sand at the water's edge. We hunkered down in Mexican style Adirondack chairs, sun bathed, talked, napped, and dreamed, and I think it was right then and there, on Maria's beach, that we decided somehow we would escape northern winters and city life and live in Mexico.

———⇒●≪———

Later that night I read the story of Alma Reed who, as Paul suspected, had been one of California's first women reporters in the '20s. As an advocate of the poor and oppressed, she assisted a Mexican family in commuting the death sentence of their son who sat on death row in San Quentin. This story was picked up by the Mexican press, and because of the publicity, the president of Mexico, Alvero Obregon, asked Reed to visit Mexico as his guest.

In her southern travels, although based in Mexico City where she reported for the Hearst newspapers, Reed was sent to Merida, in the Yucatan, to meet Dr. Edward H. Thompson, one of the leading archeologists excavating Chichen Itza. (He would later be exposed by Reed for having pilfered artifacts, jewelry, ornaments, and jade after dredging the *cenote* at Chichen Itza and sending it all to the Peabody Museum in Boston).

It was during this visit that Reed met Felipe Carrillo, the dynamic governor of the State of Yucatan. Although a married man, the charismatic Carrillo fell in love with Alma Reed, and their love story created a furor throughout Mexico and the U.S.

Carrillo wrote a romantic love song for her titled *La Peregrina*, still played by bands of serenaders today. Reed herself fueled many pages in Hearst's papers with her own romantic love story, and in the ultimate taboo, Carrillo divorced his wife of many years so he could become engaged to Alma Reed. After setting the date for their marriage, Reed hastened back to San Francisco to arrange a high profile engagement party and to wrap up her affairs before her permanent move to Mexico.

Shortly after her departure, the President of Mexico detained, then imprisoned Carrillo for his forward thinking views on how to handle a resurfacing Maya insurgency. Yucatecan land owners had developed an indentured servant status for Maya workers, who were treated as slaves. Carrillo, aiming to correct this injustice, set up vast social reforms for the Maya, including establishing the *ejido* (land grant), and translating the constitution into Maya. But there would be no storybook ending to this very public love affair. Before Reed could return from the U.S. to be at her fiance's side, he was shot before a firing squad in the Yucatan, dying a martyr's death. In Quintana Roo, the town formerly known as Chan Santa Cruz was renamed Felipe Carrillo Puerto, in honor of Carrillo.

"Well, Paul," I said as I finished up the star-crossed love affair of Alma Reed, "our new country has plenty of history, not to mention drama and romance. I want to have a really good collection of books about Mexico, so I can share them with friends and keep myself in reading material . . . search out special books like this one on the Yucatan."

"Whatever you want," Paul mumbled sleepily. He was on his way to dream land, and so was I. But my dream was of the waking variety.

That week I decided I would start collecting books, either for a personal library—the biggest in the Yucatan—or some day, a bookstore. Driven by pure love of the printed page, it didn't matter what the outcome would be. I just knew, by the time we were ready to depart for Mexico, I would have in hand thousands of books. In my southern travels I'd noticed the complete lack of bookstores anywhere in Mexico, either in Spanish or English. Years earlier, while on Isla Mujeres, I'd finished reading the books I'd brought on vacation and searched the town for a bookstore. All I could find was a sign on a locked up shop—books for sale, Wednesday, 2 to 4 p.m. I was there waiting when the proprietor opened shop that week. His inventory consisted of four pitiful boxes of worn-out paperbacks, but I found a couple that would do for beach reading. I realized then if I wanted reading material in my Mexican future, I'd best bring it myself. That's when I began collecting books.

I started hitting garage sales specifically for used books. After a preliminary pass collecting the latest pot boilers and recent best sellers, I began to search out classics, deciding to expand my horizons with a well-rounded cache of literature. Then I heard about a Friends of the Library sale taking place right in Half Moon Bay.

I'd never been to one of these sales, and had no idea how determined the crowd would be. Book dealers attended these functions and to them, this was serious business. The building was packed to near overflow and I congratulated myself on getting to the science fiction table ahead of everyone else. Having read Frank Herbert and Ray Bradbury early on, I decided I wanted to re-enter the world of science fiction, reacquaint myself with that genre.

As I stood staring at boxes of sci-fi titles, trying to read author's names and decide what to buy, a dealer swooped me by elbowing his way to the front; then he simply picked up an entire box of books, then another, then another. Science fiction, I was later to find out, was hot and difficult to find used, as many sci-fi readers were addicts and never parted with their favorites.

I was appalled. He pulled every box of books out from under my nose. I suddenly realized I was slow at the process, and better pick up speed if I planned to compete for the best books.

I meekly backed away from science fiction and dejectedly worked my way over to the travel section where there was less competition. I peered over the crowd and located Paul working his way through the art section, stacking large picture-type books, one on top of the other. At least he was having luck.

I perked up, and waded into foreign adventures. I discovered a copy of an old guide book on Mexico from the '30s, a book on the Maya by Sylvanus Morely, and a handful of traveler tales. This was fun.

A half hour later, as Paul and I merged at the checkout counter, the lady at the register asked, "Did you find everything, dear? It looks like you enjoy travel to Mexico."

"Yes, we built a house there, and now I'm on a quest to find books about Mexico, both old and new. There are no bookstores there, so I have to stock up while we're in the U.S. and bring them down with me. I'll either have the biggest home library in the Yucatan, where we've built our house, or a bookstore some day."

"Oh, Mexico. How exciting. My husband and I lived in Mexico years ago, just north of Puerto Vallarta. There were absolutely no bookstores at all down there at that time. What a wonderful idea—collecting all those books. I'd love to talk more, but it's terribly crowded." I had to agree. The line behind me was growing by the minute.

"Why don't you come in and see me next Saturday at the Friends Bookstore. If I find any books on Mexico, I'll put them aside for you."

"How nice, " I replied, "we'll do that. I'm Jeanine and this is

Paul."

"I'm Sarah, the manager. You come see me, and we'll fix you up," she said with a smile, as she started motioning to the person behind us. "We'll make sure you get your fill of Mexico, before you leave California!"

Sarah was as good as her word. With her help I gathered a unique assortment of books on Mexico. It seemed I was slowly becoming a serious collector. I was becoming a passionate pilgrim.

Almost There

The seductive song of the Mexican Caribbean charmed us. We'd been seduced by the enormous sky, clear blue waters, never-ending coastline. And whenever a serious boost was needed, little bits of magic crept in, reminders that we were still under the Caribbean's spell.

As we neared completion on the house, there was only one thing left to be finished—the façade, the outward face of the building. Paul had designed the house layout, but even in his most creative moments, he drew a blank on the exterior. So he pushed this back into Joe and Enrique's court, and asked them to sleep on it.

Amazingly, that's exactly what happened. About a week later, Enrique called, very excited. "You won't believe this!" he said. "I dreamt about your house last night, and in my dream, the façade looked like the stone structures that surround the tops of the pyramids at Chichen Itza."

He was right; I found it unbelievable . . . a dream about our house, and it looked like a pyramid?

"It looked fantastic!" he continued, his enthusiasm extending over the miles of phone line. "We'll use Mayan rock and since the roof is flat, it will add the perfect accent."

How could we say no? Then an idea came to me.

"We can call the house *Casa Maya*. It sounds as if it will look like a modern day pyramid." (In Mexico, everyone named their houses, as if they were alive. What a charming tradition).

Enrique continued, "We're going to Chichen Itza this week to take photos and study the pyramids. I'll call you when we get back. I knew I'd come up with an idea, but I never thought it would be like this!"

Enrique's dream became reality and the house's façade turned out very similar to the Temple of *Kukulkan* at Chichen Itza. Call it Maya Modern. With only five weeks left until Christmas, everything was on schedule. We were getting the best Christmas present of all.

Even though we planned on celebrating Christmas in Mexico, there was much to do in the U.S. before we left. I wrote out Christmas cards at home and at work, wrapped presents, and mailed those that required it. At the office I prepped my accounts for my absence, working later than usual and daydreaming every possible moment about paradise: a white sand beach, a translucent, turquoise sea, and doing absolutely nothing for two weeks.

After a series of non-stop Christmas parties, we reached the magic date, December 22, our day of departure.

In Mexico before NAFTA (North American Free Trade Agreement) was ratified in 1994, it was nearly impossible to find many standard issue items for building. Even simple things like switch plates or light plugs could be on back order for weeks, plus the quality on many *"hecho en Mexico"* products did not compare to what one could buy in the U.S. Because of this, our luggage was always packed to near overflow with an odd assortment of hardware.

We carried electric light switches, rheostat devices, circuit breakers, junction boxes, Halogen beach lights, toilet parts, ground fault switches, a ninety-pound voltage regulator, can openers, wine, cheese, spices, pepperoni, See's chocolates for friends, spun honey-baked hams, linens, cotton sheets, bath towels, pots and pans, radio alarm clocks, ghetto blaster, toaster, blender and more. This was just what we put in our suitcases, most which would not be declared. We had also airshipped other items too large for mere tourist travel and hoped all would be awaiting us at customs in Cancun. Of course we'd heard the infamous stories of *"la mordida,"* known as "the bite," to any gringo crazy enough to travel with more than the shirt on his or her back. Wary though we were, we were also children of the material world, and we wanted it *all*. If we couldn't buy it there, we'd haul it ourselves, thank you.

As we disembarked, the usual rush on arriving in Cancun hit us. The airport, though international, was still small in those days, and we exited the plane onto an outdoor tarmac. A wave of heat smacked me in the face as I stepped outside the air-conditioned cabin. Then came the smell, that musty, dank odor of the Yucatan and the low-lying overgrowth of jungle that seeped into the pavement on which we walked. Nothing could truly subdue it.

We had merely borrowed this land, these buildings, that tarmac. Given time, the elements, and the slightest hesitation on man's part, the jungle would again be vanquisher in this ancient pattern we'd established with nature. The smell—this emanation from the decaying jungle—was nature's way of alerting us that the battle hadn't yet been completely won . . . it was still working on a victory of its own.

We breathed it in—the jungle odor. We knew we had arrived. What's said about our fifth sense, smell? That it is the strongest of our senses, spontaneously carrying us back to moments in our personal history, identifying previous times and places in the cell block of memory.

We pushed and pulled our carry-ons towards the first line of demarcation where a secondary customs official would look us in the eye, size us up, give a small grunt, and stamp our passports. Next, we would push our carry-ons over to baggage claim and wait for the airline staff to do their share of retrieval, moving parcels and suitcases from gurney to conveyor belt.

Mexico customs had developed an egalitarian system for baggage inspection of incoming passengers. One simply pushed a button attached to an apparatus that looked like a traffic light. It would read either red or green—there was no mistaking what course would be taken once the light was triggered. Green meant freedom and on with your vacation. You were free to frolic in the ocean, dance at Coco Bongo, drink margaritas till dawn. Let the games begin! Red meant some over-zealous official with prodding hands and a certainty of purpose—your contraband— would rifle through your personal effects while scores of others—tourists and bean counters alike—looked on.

We weren't one hundred percent certain the button pushing was a random effort at checking bags. I'd noticed on more than one occasion the poor slob standing dejectedly at the customs checkpoint with underwear and other assorted items—camera, shampoo, jeans, deodorant—strewn everywhere, was more often than not a long-hair with a beard and backpack. Were backpacks a barometer to customs agents of the world? Branding those carrying them as the likes of the troublesome traveler?

After countless trips to Mexico we developed our own atmospheric pressure guide for sailing through customs. We waited until someone pushed a red light, and immediately dashed for that check point, as red lights were the exception. So it was much to my amazement that day at Cancun International when I pushed the button and the light flashed red. Paul cleared customs just moments before with a green light on the meter next to mine, and was already in the safety zone on the other side, locating a porter.

"Take your things to that table," instructed a young woman in uniform who stood at the counter, already eyeing me suspiciously.

I gazed in trepidation at the customs' debriefing area, and stared down into the eyes of a customs midget. Hand to God, the man was no more than four feet tall.

Am I hallucinating? I wondered. Let's see. I had two drinks on the plane, and our flight was really early, maybe . . . I blinked twice and looked again. No, there was actually a dwarf in uniform right in front of me, bandying a small baton from one hand to the other. Apparently he had plans for it; he would use it to shuffle through my things, like a cleaner version of the white glove test. *Ay, chihuahua!* I was headed for trouble!

"*Buenas tardes.*" Good afternoon, I gamely began, as he pushed and pulled my numerous pieces of baggage closer to his check point. They were bigger than he was, no doubt about it. Actually, they were bigger than me.

"*Buenas tardes,*" he replied, with a glint in his eye.

I felt he was defying me to give him the once-over, for size, but I was too politically correct for that. Well, what could I do? I was forced to play the hand I'd been dealt by the red button. I decided to act as pleasant as possible throughout the ordeal.

"Ready for Christmas?" I asked, trying for perfect Spanish pronunciation.

He eyed me tentatively and nodded with a curt, "*Sí.*" Then he seemed to reconsider and asked, in hesitating English, "Where are you from?"

"California," I replied. For some reason, when asked this question of location in Mexico, California is always the right place to be from, probably because so many Mexicans have family there, legally or otherwise.

"Hollywood?" he pressed, with a devilish grin.

"No, San Francisco, but I know Hollywood."

While we engaged in this verbal exchange, he slowly began to rustle through my luggage and with sure, swift movements began working his way into the heart of darkness, the center of my suitcase. What evil contraband he would find, I wasn't sure. By this time, even *I* couldn't remember what purloined objects I'd put where.

I winced as I saw his baton fondle a stick of pepperoni (no meat products!), dawdle over my honey baked ham, and move on. He caressed my Halogen light, pretending it did not exist, and then motioned towards bag number two.

"Do you know Rambo?" he asked, eyeing me again.

"Sylvester Stallone? No, but I know his movies," I answered demurely.

By this time he was well into my second suitcase, again dancing all around my belongings. As I watched in horror, I realized there was nothing in the suitcase that *wasn't* contraband! My God! Hadn't I declared *anything?*

"Next," he stated, as he aptly pushed aside my taboo valise, pretending he hadn't seen the voltage regulators, the radio alarm clock, the blender.

We were moving onto bag number three and back into the name game.

"Schwarzennager?" he demanded, holding his baton authoritatively, like a conductor's wand. "Do you know *him?*"

"No, but he is, *como se dice,* how do you say it? A real dude? *En español?*"

"Duuuuude?" the pint-sized agent asked.

"You know, *que hombre!* What a guy!" I gushed.

By that time, I was feeling a little lightheaded. I don't know if it was the heat, the agony of being stopped, the dwarf agent, the overall weirdness. I knew I was over-reacting, but I couldn't help it. For a moment I glimpsed Paul in the safety zone of the free world on the other side of the customs terminal. He was helplessly watching my mini-horror flick unfold. I caught other tourists giving me sidelong glances as they wheeled their respectable, untampered luggage through the turnstiles, into a waiting crowd of tour guides and porters. The promised land.

"Arnold . . . Schwarzenneger!" the customs dwarf announced the name a second time, like a battle cry. *"Terminator!"* By this time he'd reached my last bag. He handled it gently, holding the baton under his chin as he carefully opened the latch and took a perfunctory look inside.

I could tell he wasn't going to fine me, detain me, or trouble me in any way at all. Why? When my bags were rife with contraband?

We'd stumbled onto a universal maxim, he and I. It was as simple as that—the movies, Hollywood, a common denominator in our global village. In his poorly rendered English and in my fractured Spanish, we discovered a language in which we were both fluent.

As he pushed aside my last bag and closed it with a demonstrative thump, he gave me one last look.

"Okay, then. You remember, '*Hasta la vista*,' baby? Who said it?"

I burst out laughing, "Schwarzenneger! *Hasta la vista*, baby, *a usted! Y Feliz Navidad!"*

Paul had watched this entire production in somber silence. I had seen him physically cringe a couple of times as he stood on tiptoe to view the contemptible, illegal products the customs agent had come across in my suitcase. He smiled a big one at me from his safe haven where he'd secured a porter who would soon whisk us out to the unforgiving afternoon heat . . . and freedom.

La Mordida

Once outside, I breathed a sigh of relief. I was beginning to feel like Xena, warrior princess, each moment a new battle. Could I continue to slay the dragons? Now came our true trial—the real customs agents—the airport boys, known for their vile moods and sleight of hand. The agents at the arrival gates were known to be notoriously loose, my own recent experience proving that to be true. Agents from the customs office wore the badges, walked the walk, talked the talk.

We told the porter the name of our car rental company and followed him to the pick-up area, secured our car, and drove with apprehension to the air freight terminal to see if our goods had arrived. The next test.

Within a few moments, a Mexicana clerk told us our packages had arrived in Cancun, so we headed immediately to customs to fill out paperwork and retrieve the boxes. Since the holidays approached, we knew the sooner the better for any pick-ups we might have. In Mexico, most government offices closed for at least two weeks around the Christmas holidays and we were nearing that deadline.

We pulled our car into a cramped parking area, and entered enemy territory. Mexican government offices never failed me in their barrenness. I gazed in horror at the overall deterioration of the building, realizing it was only a few years old. The gun metal gray of the cement exterior perfectly suited the somber attitude I found inside. We went to the front counter and I asked who could assist us in retrieving our Mexicana air freight.

"I am the proper person. Papers?" an office wonk said, as he peered at me over narrow, wire frame glasses. What is it with government officials of the world? Do they all exude ennui in epidemic proportions, no matter what their ages?

"Yes," he nodded, looking over our list. "These items are here. If you don't pick them up today you will have to wait until January 4." He pushed the paperwork back over the counter towards me.

"Today is good," I replied, slowly inching the paperwork back in his direction.

"Well, then, you'll need to go to Cancun and find a customs broker who can fill everything out for you. I'll give you a list of names and addresses," he said, reaching for a file brimming with papers that looked seriously out of order. He watched our faces fall, adjusted his glasses, and continued; now that he had our attention he could go in for the kill.

"Or, if you would like to take care of everything right here, maybe we can make some arrangements."

Of course, by arrangements he was referring to a bribe.

Paul spoke up quickly, "That would be fine. What do we need to do?"

"Just follow me," the wonk said with a crooked smile, and he started walking briskly from behind the desk towards an exit sign.

We followed him through a maze of lone desks accompanied by decrepit office chairs and ancient Underwood typewriters down a narrow hallway to the back of a sprawling warehouse which served as a holding tank.

Behind a formidable screened-in section, securely locked, we could see assorted boxes, crates, pallets, what-have-you. But none of it looked the least bit orderly. In fact, it was the messiest warehouse I had ever seen. It hardly looked like government property. Some boxes displayed contents already thoroughly mangled, other boxes were broken with items sticking out the top and sides. Puddles of water appeared in places and uncollected goods showed signs of water damage. Other areas had debris strewn up and down the dusty, concrete floor. I had to surmise all these goods belonged to someone, and they hadn't started out in such deplorable condition.

On one side of the room sat five pallets clearly stamped with a well-known frozen dessert trademark, in large, unmistakable lettering. The contents had been uncrated from the container it had arrived in, and was left unrefrigerated while awaiting customs clearance. More good planning, I thought, as I watched the syrupy, once frozen product drip onto an already seriously soiled floor.

If just one corner of this enormous warehouse had been in disarray, it might have passed as an indiscretion. But the negligence spread throughout the entire holding tank. Frankly, the entire place was a shambles.

"I can't believe this is the government customs agency," I whispered to Paul as we waited for the agent to unlock the fenced-off area.

Our customs agent ushered us in, closed the wire fence behind us, and quickly picked up his gait. As he moved towards a pallet with Mexicana-stamped cartons and boxes, he let out a low, sharp whistle. Immediately I saw a young dock worker sprint towards us from one of the side aisles, ready to assist.

Within moments the boxes on the Mexicana pallet were rearranged and there they were—our air freight containers. In a few minutes, the agent tallied things on paper, then in his head, and came up with a figure.

His lean form curved forward in a conciliatory gesture as he spoke, "Fifty U.S., and it's ready to go now." His tone was low and conspiratorial.

"Fine," Paul said, like a pro, reaching for his wallet. "Here you go," and he extended his hand with a crisp, new bill to the agent.

But our wonk was already on the move, pretending he had never seen us, had never entered the back of the warehouse, and had no idea who we were or where we came from.

Quick as a Yucatec lizard catching an unsuspecting fly, the warehouse worker moved in, accepted the money, then began to move our boxes off the pallet, carrying them towards the gate. We dutifully followed behind, amazed at the education we received each time our feet touched Mexican soil.

As the worker helped us load our boxes into the rental car, another man with a clipboard came up, gazed into the vehicle, asked for our papers. We handed him our copies, he looked them over, nodded and walked towards the parking area. Assuming we'd cleared customs, we started the car and cruised towards the gate. At the gatekeeper's tower we were stopped again, scrutinized along with our boxes, and finally waved on. It was the last checkpoint between us and the road. Checks and balances, the Mexican motto.

"Whew! What an ordeal! But we're home free. *Feliz Navidad!*" I shouted as Paul gunned the gasping four cylinder engine. We were finally on Highway 307 heading towards Puerto Morelos.

—————>●<—————

The twenty minute drive south to Puerto Morelos always brought me peace of mind. Once past the mandatory army check point near the airport turnoff, the two lane road narrowed and the low, green jungle dominated the landscape. It was truly a pastoral scene, with only the pavement to remind me that I was connected to something. There were no billboards, no road signs, no street lights, no fences.

When first we traveled to the Yucatan, I had expected a different type of rain forest. I thought the trees would be tall as redwoods with bright flowers—bromeliads and orchids everywhere, maybe flocks of parrots, and, of course, monkeys.

These were the basic components of the Yucatan tropical rain forest, but as the Costa Maya became more populated, I had to travel farther off the beaten track to find this. To see extremely tall, tropical hardwoods, I went inland, off the coast route and into Chiapas or southern Campeche, a few hours away. There one could view redwood size tropical hardwoods with buttresses extending outward like gigantic, cloved hooves, eliciting a feeling of having stumbled onto a fairy wonderland. Howler monkeys lived in these yet uncut primordial forests behind the pyramids at Palenque and in the wilderness area surrounding Calakmul.

There was an earthy solitude to the northern Yucatan's lowlying jungle where we were. This feeling took hold as soon as the road turned southward. Then came the big sky—so big the Mayans called it *Sian Ka'an* or "where the sky is born." The clouds here were always large and billowy, beyond Maxfield Parish, but at day's end, in the same palate of colors. I drew in a breath or sighed, taking it all in; I'm not sure which. Paul looked over at me and smiled.

"You're very close to seeing your Christmas present—a brand new house!"

"Very close," I responded, with a satisfied smile as we passed Crococun, the crocodile farm, just a few miles from the Morelos turnoff. Then before I knew it, we were at the crossroads by the Pemex station, turning onto the narrow road into Puerto Morelos.

The next kilometers crawled by. Finally we were on the washboard beach road, driving to our new house, *Casa Maya*.

At last we saw it.

Pulling into the driveway, made from Mayan rock left from Barry's house before the hurricane, I saw the finished product. The mahogany door was wrapped like a Christmas present, with an ample red velvet bow, as large as the door itself. Just atop the entryway was an effigy of a Mayan god painted white with a long hook extending out in a curve.

An air of mystery embraced the house thanks to the façade that simulated a Mayan pyramid, just as Enrique had promised. As we exited the rental car, Enrique popped his head out the door and shouted, *"Feliz Navidad!"*

"It's incredible, and it looks like Chichen Itza! I love it! What Mayan god have you placed atop our entryway, Enrique?"

"Chac, Rain God. In all the Maya hierarchy, he is the most powerful, because the Yucatan is a place with no rivers. Rain here is a blessing."

Having read new statistics that Quintana Roo may have experienced a century long drought, sometime between 700 and 900 A.D., I agreed with Enrique. Rain in Quintana Roo *is* a blessing.

"Bienvenidos!" Joe Marino said, standing slightly behind Enrique. "Are you getting the Cliff's Notes version of Maya Gods? Welcome!"

The next half hour was like a dream as we walked from room to room, cooing in unison about the quality of the workmanship, the dynamics of the house, the views. We noticed it all—the mahogany everywhere, the built-in bookshelves, Mexican tile floors, niches for Maya art. A great deal of the finish work had been done with little direction from Paul and me, which clearly showed the amount of initiative Joe and Enrique used when a design decision needed to be made and we were thousands of miles away. The finished product couldn't have been better.

So, this is *Casa Maya*, I thought. It did seem like it had taken a millennium to reach this lovely culmination, but that was the nine hundred and ninety nine years *before* we met Joe Marino and Enrique. Their portion of the project took precisely one year to complete, exactly as planned. And it came in on time and on budget. In Mexico, of all places.

That night after Joe and Enrique left and Paul had fallen asleep, I crept back into the living room of our new house. While still in San Francisco I bought a special incense from a store in the Mission that sold religious items for churches. I had two heart-shaped candles I'd also saved for this occasion, and in front of the living room window facing the vast Caribbean, I prepared a makeshift altar. The house needed a blessing.

Who do I pray to? I asked myself as I began lighting the incense and candles. As the musky odor of incense drifted throughout the room, a night breeze picked up off the ocean, and the candles began to flicker.

It will come to me . . . *Chac*!

"*Chac*, God of Rain, bless *Casa Maya*, and keep it safe. *Ixchel*, Mother Goddess, bless this house and make it a safe place for all who come here."

I remained there for a time, feeling grateful to the gods that allowed me to culminate my journey into the land of the Maya, and first and foremost, for allowing it to take place.

———⸭———

The rains did not start immediately; they waited until the following day, Christmas Eve, to begin. But they lasted for three full days and nights. I kept asking myself, what *exactly* did I say to *Chac*, Rain God?

When visitors come to *Casa Maya* and ask about the effigy of *Chac* above our entryway, I tell the story of the Rain God, how the house was built in his honor, and how he showed his gratitude by letting the skies pour down rain for three solid days at Christmastime, years earlier. His blessing on *Casa Maya*.

Day Tripping

Knowing *Casa Maya* was a fait accompli was a gift in itself. In the days that followed, we were busy with shopping trips to Cancun and getting things settled at the house. We organized dishes, pots and pans in the pantry; assigned closets for bed linens and towels; and learned to wash all fruits and vegetables with a few drops of Microdyne in a quart of water, which cleansed them of all bacteria.

We ordered top soil for the front yard so we could plant palm trees, shrubs, bougainvillea. Although the house was complete, the surrounding area was starkly bare, and we wanted to add as much foliage as possible. We decided to maximize the concept of *Casa Maya* by searching for Mayan-style artwork and incorporating it into both the interior and exterior of the house. We knew the region near Valladolid had plenty of stone masons who created knockoff artifacts that looked just like the *stellae*, or stone tablets, at the pyramid sites. After New Year's, we'd take a day trip to see what we could find.

By mid-week, the rains had subsided and we lolled around the beach for a few days, enjoying the sun, the sand and the quiet. Occasionally a neighbor would greet us on the beach to wish us happy holidays or simply to chat. Some days we'd wade in the warm Caribbean water up to our knees, other days we snorkeled just offshore, amazed at the number of fish and conch we'd see.

We'd celebrated Christmas Eve with Joe Marino, Enrique, and their families, and planned to reciprocate by hosting a New

Year's Eve party to show our appreciation for a job well done and to christen *Casa Maya*. We invited everyone we knew from town and all the people who had worked on the house. Arturo planned to come from Merida and bring his guitar. Apparently carpentry wasn't his only talent.

New Year's Eve proved to be quite a fiesta. Paul and I had cooked all day, my forte being appetizers, salsas, desserts and an assorted variety of Christmas cookies I made every year, no matter what land I was in. Paul took on the more difficult matters of the main course—he was the meat and potatoes man. We opted to serve the purloined honey baked ham I'd smuggled past customs agents at the airport, along with a roast turkey complete with Paul's delicious dressing and giblet gravy. What we couldn't eat, we'd send home with our guests.

Arturo brought along a friend for backup vocals, and all I remembered of the evening was a beautiful seranade of song. Another thing I loved about Mexico—everyone knew the words to countless verses of numerous songs. They all sang together and no one held back; everyone joined in. We ate, sang, and partied until 4 a.m. What a night and what an inauguration for *Casa Maya*.

New Year's Day brought sun. We slept late and finally dragged ourselves out of bed to face the day-after-the-fiesta clean-up. We opened all the windows, let fresh Caribbean breezes blow through, put music on the cassette deck, and broke open another bottle of champagne for our private work party. By late afternoon everything was back to normal and we fixed ourselves sandwiches, happily content that we'd successfully survived our first Mexican fiesta in our own home. To change the pace, we decided to take a walk into Puerto Morelos by way of the beach. A wide expanse of nothingness stretched from our house to town in those days. It was near sunset, and the sun sank over the mangroves to the west, not over the ocean as we were accustomed to in California. The reflection of sunset on the water was something to behold, creating a pinkish backdrop of color projected onto billowy clouds.

Carrying our sandals, we walked barefoot on the beach, arriving at the town square just as the mercury vapor lights came on at the basketball court. Several teens passed the ball back and forth without much enthusiasm as we took a seat on the concrete park benches next to a family of four. The parents were 40-something, with two pre-teen daughters, and we fell into conversation about the game, the day, and their recent travels.

Just back from Valladolid, they'd seen the little known pyramids at Ek Balam. Since we planned a trip in that direction the very next day, we were curious about the site, knowing nothing about it.

"Ek Balam is only twenty minutes north of Valladolid. There's a small marker pointing directions at the town square," the father told us. "There was no one there when we visited the site. We walked through fields and then there we were—in the midst of all these temples, barely uncovered. Some excavation has been done, though. We ran into an archeologist and he said it was a major site and had probably been inhabited for close to one thousand years, from 100 B.C. to 700 A.D. He said they need more funding, and he was running a skeletal crew.

"One building, the archeologist told us, was one of the largest Mayan structures in the Yucatan. He called it the Acropolis, over five hundred feet long," he continued.

"It means bright star jaguar. Ek Balam," one of the girls said, taking an interest in the conversation. She was about thirteen, and her blond hair had been braided in tight corn rows. "Jaguars are powerful in the Maya world."

"How fascinating," I said, now excited about the prospect of doing some exploring at the ruins. "We'll be driving through Valladolid tomorrow, so maybe we'll take time to stop and see what we can see."

Paul nodded his head in agreement and said, "Sounds like it will be a long day. I suppose we should head back to the house and get packed for our road trip. Nice meeting you, and thanks for the information."

"I hope you have a good trip, wherever you end up," I said, as we waved good bye.

We started back towards the beach, ready for our ten minute trek to the house. A half moon rose in the winter sky. Stars peeked out from the darkened heavens, brilliant and bright. I searched for the Pleiades constellation, the Seven Sisters from Greek mythology, daughters of Atlas who were placed by Zeus amongst the stars.

"Look at the stars, Paul," I said, as we picked our way carefully along the darkened beach, wading between sand and surf. "They're so bright. I see the Pleiades; and there's Orion's Belt."

"It *is* dark out here; the stars are incredible. Makes you wonder, doesn't it? Seeing those far away stars?" he commented.

"Mmm-hmm," I agreed. "Those stars, the blue colored stars like in the Pleiades, are around five hundred light years from earth. Blows my mind."

"So by the time that light reaches us, maybe those stars don't exist. Any way you look at it, though, I've never seen brighter stars or a darker sky than right here in Puerto Morelos," he marveled.

He was right about that. Puerto Morelos was so small at that time, there was no peripheral lighting to diminish the stars' brightness. Once away from the town square, it was incredibly dark, creating the perfect backdrop for a spectacular night sky.

At that moment, our minds were on the stars, but tomorrow

we'd be well out of the clouds, firmly grounded in a different reality—the jungles of the Yucatan, searching for different answers to different mysteries. We were going to the pyramids at Ek Balam.

———>••<———

To a Californian, sunrise on the Atlantic seems a contradiction after watching the sun set on the opposite shore of the Pacific day after day for years. It takes some getting used to. But what a display. As the sky starts to take on light, a haze of soft color permeates the horizon. Then the orange-red sliver appears, flush with the ocean, not round at all. And slowly the great ball of flame surfaces. Another day.

Paul and I were already up. I was arranging clothes in a small duffel bag, drinking a quick cup of coffee before we got on the road. Paul finished putting juice, water, sodas, and ice into a cooler. "Are you ready?" he asked, waiting for me at the front door.

"Let's go," I said, following him outside into the quiet morning, checking the lock as we left.

———>••<———

Valladolid was a Yucatan city with a disastrous history. Not unlike Atlanta of the Old South, it crashed and burned, but in a slow motion debacle that lasted three centuries. The city was founded in 1543 by the nephew of Francisco de Montejo, conqueror of the Yucatan. Montejo gave his nephew sovereignty over lands to the east of Merida, and the nephew explored the area, making his base next to a lagoon called Chouac-Ha. He named the new city Valladolid and authorized land grants to forty-five Spaniards, displacing the indigenous Mayans who already lived there. In what would become a continuous cycle, the Spaniards subjugated local Mayan tribes, and constantly battled them for dominion as they rose up in rebellion. Then the Spaniards crushed the rebellions, and the Mayans rose again, culminating in 1847 in the bloody massacre known as the Caste War of the Yucatan which killed 250,000. "Paul, you won't believe this history," I said as I shifted positions in the front seat of our rental car. "We're heading straight into the heart of Maya land."

From what I was reading in *The Caste War of Yucatan*, by Nelson Reed, no single element alone instigated the rebellion, but as in most revolutions, a long dominated underclass was finally pushed to the limit by an overbearing uberclass that performed intolerable deeds. Indentured servitude, land grabbing, and water rights were a few of the issues that pushed the Maya into full-fledged revolt.

Valladolid was the most elitist and race conscious city in the Yucatan. After a decade of skirmishes, in 1847, when local Mayans heard one of their leaders had been put to death by firing squad, they rose up and marched on Valladolid, hacking eighty-five people to death by machete, burning, raping, and pillaging. Merida was sure to be the next staging ground for what was fast becoming a race war. In retaliation for the Valladolid massacre, the Yucatecans descended on the ranch of a Mayan leader and raped a twelve-year old Indian girl. With this affront, eight Maya tribes joined forces and drove the entire elite population of Yucatan to Merida, burning towns and pillaging as they went. So fierce was the slaughter that all non-Maya prepared to evacuate Merida and the peninsula by boat.

But just as the Mayan tribes approached Merida, sure of victory, fate intervened when great clouds of winged ants appeared in the sky. With this first sign of rain coming, the Maya knew it was time to begin planting. They laid down their machetes and headed home to their cornfields. It was time to plant corn, a thing as simple and ancient as that.

In 1848 the Yucatecans staged a comeback, killed Mayan leaders, and reunified. This fighting would continue well into the twentieth century, for over sixty years. A three century struggle, begun in 1543 when Montejo's nephew subjugated those early Mayans, did not truly end until 1915 with the Mexican Revolution. At that time, one of Mexico's generals canceled all debt labor, freeing 60,000 Mayans and their families of 350 years of indentured servitude. But until the 1900's, the Caste War of the Yucatan made it impossible for any light skinned person to walk into the eastern Yucatan or Quintana Roo and come out alive.

⟶➤●◄⟵

We were on the paid highway just outside of Valladolid. As we stopped at the toll booth and deposited money with the toll taker, the monotonous landscape of the eastern Yucatan prevailed. Flat and dry, with occasional *cecropia*, or trumpet trees, the infrequent fenced farm with a small hacienda was all there was to see. In five minutes, we were at the outskirts of the city, driving on a narrow one-way street, past small cement block houses. A mustard-yellow stone wall hugged the road all the way into *el centro*.

An erect traffic cop, dressed in brown uniform with white gloves, directed cars forward in swift, confident movements. A shiny steel whistle hung from his neck, but he didn't seem to need it. Our rental car bolted forward towards the square, alive with people. Girls sold handkerchiefs near the central garden; women sold *huipiles*, the embroidered white Mayan dress still popular in the Yucatan today; and vendors at soft drink stands sold sodas in plastic bags with straws. Wrought iron benches with wooden slats were filled with an assortment of people, some locals, some tourists. I gazed at an ancient, lovely stone church with two tall spires that stood on the south corner of the square as we rounded the wide traffic circle, looking for the sign that would direct us to Ek Balam.

Although its past history was ominous, present day Valladolid was that pleasant contradiction one so commonly finds in Mexico—a busy city with one foot in the past, and one in the future. Commerce prevailed, and the streets were lined with shoppers and vendors taking care of daily chores and business.

Intrigued by the bustle, the charm, and the colonial architecture of Valladolid, we parked the car in front of the Hotel *Meson de Marques* to have breakfast and a quick look around before touring Ek Balam. Although a sign announced a breakfast buffet at the hotel, there was a wide, open-air arcade next door that intrigued us. On either side small lunch and breakfast spots served up fast food, and an abundance of metal card tables with chairs proliferated throughout the center walkway. Waiters hawked seats at the tables, holding menus in hand, pleading for our business. We sat down at a neat enamel table with a bright blue Corona bottle—*no mas fina*—no other finer—painted full center.

"*Desayuno?*" the waiter asked. Breakfast?

"*Por supuesto,*" I responded. Of course.

One of the joys of colonial Yucatan was having a break from the sky-high prices found on the coast. Paul and I enjoyed a delicious Mexican breakfast for pesos and sauntered off a half hour later, ready to explore the pyramids at Ek Balam.

One more time around the traffic circle and *el centro*, and we spotted the sign directing us to the pyramid site, only fifteen kilometers away. Another one-way street led out of town, and we followed it past small pharmacies, neat houses, and the occasional *tienda*, or market. Once on the city's outskirts, the road narrowed considerably, but was smooth and newly paved. Another sign, several kilometers later, pointed to the right, and we took a turn that dipped and led down to an empty creek bed, and then back up the other side into a small forgotten *pueblo*. Packed dirt streets no more than twelve feet wide were bordered by rock walls dividing the street from tiny yards with ancient stone houses, some coated with rough plaster. At one crossroads, two squealing pink piglets ran dangerously close to our wheels, chased by a squawking red rooster, tail feathers bobbing. An old woman, hunched over from years of manual labor or lack of calcium, eyed our late model rent-a-car cautiously as we inched our way through this time warp in history.

Finally out of town, we welcomed the freedom of the open countryside. In the distance I saw a pyramid temple peeking above the low shrub landscape.

A simple green sign with an arrow and picture of a pyramid pointed down a side road to the north. We turned onto the *sacbe*, as the Maya called these ancient pathways, and drove slowly towards what we hoped was the site entrance. At a primitive twig *palapa* a caretaker appeared. He explained there was a ten peso donation, and asked if we wanted a guide. We said yes, and he pointed to a raven-haired boy of ten, "*Mi hijo,* Jorge." George, his son, would assist us. We dropped the pesos in a handmade wooden box, and followed the boy down the *sacbe*.

Except for his size, Jorge had all the attributes of a serious forty-year old. He was reflective, deliberate in his speech, and very smart. As we walked, he began telling us the history of Ek Balam. Founded around 100 B.C., the site was named for a Mayan ruler, Ek Balam, bright star jaguar. *Ek* to the Mayans was the brightest star in the heavens; *balam* was the word for jaguar. The first excavations of the site were carried out by Frenchman Desire Charnay in 1886, and recent work had begun in 1987 when INAH (National Institute of Anthropology and History) funding was granted. Although the city was compact, there was still much to be done. He explained that the number of buildings on the site suggested Ek Balam had been rich and powerful at the same time, possibly holding the position of agricultural center of the northwestern Yucatan.

We walked through an amazing four-sided gateway arch that, Jorge explained, connected to a *sacbe*, or road, which connected all the Mayan kingdoms. Ek Balam had numerous *sacbes*, he told us, to all the major sites in the northern Yucatan and beyond. The views from the gateway arch were breathtaking.

"Paul," I remarked, "this is fantastic!"

A three-sided wall, either ceremonial or defensive, was built around the city, similar to the wall at Tulum. Ek Balam was known to contain an astrological observatory, a palace, a tower, a ball court, two *cenotes*, and a building archeologists named the Acropolis, most likely due to the sculptures found inside—full figure statues that looked more Greek than Maya.

From the ten-foot high stairway at the gateway arch, Jorge directed us through the ball court and onward to the remarkable Acropolis. He told us the Acropolis was twice the size of *El Castillo* at Chichen Itza, with tunnels inside leading to the tombs. A unique stucco fresco had life-size statues intricately carved into it. These were definitely unique in the Maya world. They appeared almost Asian, closer to Cambodia's Angor Wat than Chichen Itza. It was like nothing I had ever seen in Mexico.

We climbed two-thirds of the way up the edifice, to get a closer look at the remarkable statues. Burnished by time to a golden brown, it was almost impossible to believe they were here in Ek Balam. Paul stood before the stucco fresco. "They seem Grecian, or Indian. Look at the lotus position, on that statue," he said as he pointed at a character with a Shiva-style headdress.

Through a hallway, leading to the tomb of the ruler Ukit Kan Le'k Tok, founder of the Ek Balam dynasty, was a twelve-foot high stucco mouth with teeth, representing the gateway to the underworld, the Maya version of the River Styxx. Archeologists theorize most of the Acropolis was built around 800 A.D. by Ukit Kan Lek Tok.

The Maya so well preserved the stucco in the Acropolis tomb that no modern restoration was required. After the ruler was buried, the tomb was filled with powdered limestone and rocks, and the entire facade was covered with the same material, for preservation.

Jorge was a perfect guide, very absorbed in the details of the site and its history. He confided that his dream was to become an archeologist some day. We paid him for his guide work and he followed us out to the car, not wanting to end the conversation.

Within minutes he became a ten-year old again, excitedly asking where we were from and where we were going. He gallantly opened my car door, and in doing so, spotted my *Mayan Ruins Guide* in the back seat.

Noticing his look of longing, I asked, *"Quieres mi libro?"* Would you like my book?

"Si, si!" he exclaimed, looking terribly excited at the prospect.

I told him it was in English, but I was sure that since he was going to be a famous archeologist some day, he would soon learn to read and speak English.

He agreed with me wholeheartedly, and the last image I have of Jorge was his hugging the *Mayan Ruins Guide* tightly to his chest as we pulled onto the ancient *sacbe* leading us away from Ek Balam.

Of Rulers and Kings

We followed the ancient road back to the small *pueblo* where we'd seen the squealing piglets, backtracking all the way to Valladolid. Once in that city, we looked for the *"libre"* free road, that would wind thirty miles to Chichen Itza. It was on this road that stone masons lived and worked and sold their crafts. In my mind, I imagined they were ancestors of the mighty builders of the pyramids at Chichen Itza, and why wouldn't they be? Skills were passed from generation to generation, especially with builders in Mexico. Since education took a back seat to livelihood, many men followed in their fathers' footsteps, especially in the building professions.

Topes were plentiful on the *libre* road. We called them Mayan speed bumps, slowing us down as we traveled through small towns, past children playing outside *palapa* huts and women sweeping packed dirt doorsteps with brooms of straw. Back in the countryside, we drove past *milpas,* ancient Mayan corn fields, and a few farms with Brahma cattle grazing in lush green fields. Onward to Chichen Itza.

In about an hour we passed the Chichen Itza airport, then came the entrance to the pyramids. We kept driving towards Piste, the small access village that swelled with hotels, restaurants and shops playing host to the burgeoning tourist trade. Just before we approached town, I spotted several *stellae,* Maya stone tablets, in front of a stucco house, propped against tall trees for support. In the background, two feathered vision serpents, like those at Chichen Itza's *El Castillo*, looked eerily real with their mouths gaping wide open.

"Paul, stop!" I said. "We've got to look at those tablets." The Maya carved stone tablets to commemorate events, and displayed them at the pyramid sites. They were sizable, about three feet high, and half a foot wide. Many were corroded, ruined by time and the elements.

Paul pulled the car onto the berm of the paved road, directly alongside the stone tablets. Our arrival brought a handsome brown-haired man of thirty, the artist, out the front door. He smiled at us, noticing our excitement at seeing these life-size Maya *stellae*.

The artist's name was Alfonso. He asked us to come inside the house which was set up like a rustic gallery. Glazed vases, Maya figurines, intricate stone pieces, sat on dark wooden shelves around the wall's perimeter. Sitting at a burl table, cut from ancient mahogany, was an older Mayan, Alfonso's father. We asked about the *stellae*, and why they looked so authentic. Alfonso grabbed an oversized, water- damaged book from one of the shelves, and started leafing through it. It was an art book from the University of Oklahoma, with two hundred pages of Maya art pieces in full color prints. Alfonso explained how he drew a precise copy from the book, carved a mold, and poured the piece. After this process was done, he pulled the mold off, and added an ochre-colored paint glaze to the finished piece, giving it the look of antiquity. He was right about that. It looked very real and very old. His artwork was perfect for *Casa Maya*.

Alfonso's interest in Maya art came from his father. The older man had worked as an apprentice for archeologist Alberto Ruz years ago. Ruz was the Mexican archeologist who discovered the hidden tomb that housed the sarcophagus of Pacal, Palenque's greatest leader, along with his jeweled death mask. This discovery by Ruz in 1952 was considered one of the most notable recent archeological achievements in the Maya world. Although Palenque's Temple of Inscriptions, which houses the tomb, had previously been investigated by others, Ruz found that the inner walls of the temple did not end at the junction with the floor, but continued on below it.

Noticing holes in one large floor slab, Ruz deduced they were finger holds, thus believing the pyramid on which the temple stood might have another structure concealed inside. As he suspected, the slab, when lifted, revealed a stairway, but it was blocked with rubble. He instructed his crew to clear it and this took nearly three years. His efforts, however, were richly rewarded when the stairway ended in one of the most elaborate tombs ever discovered in Mesoamerica—the tomb of Pacal. To this day visitors may still descend down the very steps cleared by Ruz's team and view the sarcophagus lid of this Mayan ruler. Ruz was so closely linked to his discovery that he is buried right there at Palenque in front of the Temple of Inscriptions, a stone's throw from the tomb of Pacal.

Alfonso's father's interest in archeology had spilled onto his son, and both were well-versed in Maya art and culture, easily explaining which *stellae* belonged to which sites. It was a fascinating hour we spent with them, looking through the art book and commenting on different Mayan art pieces, and then having a story told about that particular object. We bought the large *stellae* which was a replica of the Rearing Vision Serpent, from Yaxchilan. Yaxchilan was a Maya site not far from Palenque, on the Usumacinta River in Chiapas. Alfonso had also made a small cement-like statue of reclining god Chac Mool, and Paul thought it would look nice in the back yard, once things were planted. Getting Chac Mool plus the meter-high *stellae*, at two-hundred pounds, into our car took some arranging, but we managed, and after giving Alfonso a hefty stack of pesos, we were on our way, promising to come back again for more artwork.

By this time it was late in the day and with our heavy load, we decided to stop over at Chichen Itza for the night. The Hacienda Chichen Hotel was the original 1923 headquarters for the Carnegie Institution's Maya Archeological Expedition, including the likes of archeologists Sylvanus Morley, who excavated the site for nearly thirty years, and Dr. Edward Thompson, who as U.S. Consul to the Yucatan in 1890, purchased the pyramid site, as the ruins had no protected status at that time, and started excavating. Thompson also infamously dredged the sacred *cenote*, sending artifacts back to the U.S. Years later, some of these artifacts were returned to Mexico and many today are on display in Mexico City's Museum of Anthropology.

Authentic Mayan temple stones were used to build the hacienda, which first operated as a cattle ranch in the 16th century, and one hundred years later as a sisal (or henequen) plantation. The Yucatan was known to have approximately five hundred working haciendas during the henequen boom when Panama hats became fashionable at the turn of the century. Hacienda Chichen itself was a large rambling structure with long welcoming porch and sixteen-foot ceilings done in Spanish-style architecture. Potted ferns and banana trees in immense Mexican pots sat on Mayan flagstone rock. Colonial style rocking chairs with wicker backing were lined up near the entrance. Decorated with stone sculptures and Mayan artwork, the ambience was complete—a charming blend of Mexican colonial and Maya culture. I felt as if I'd stepped back in time. On the grounds, cottages had been built in the '20s for the Carnegie archeology staff, and at that time Dr. Thompson had planted fruit and flowering trees for a Mayan style garden. Hacienda Chichen was just the place to relax for a night before heading back to the coast.

The hacienda sat right on the pyramid site, and since we were there, we decided to take in the evening sound and light show at Chichen Itza. Performances were given in three languages, English, Spanish, and German. The show was spectacular, lasting an hour, with tales of warlike rulers, priests, and Mayan gods backed up by dramatic colored light displays on the various pyramid structures. *Fantastico,* the only word to describe it.

We made our way back to Hacienda Chichen, had a delicious dinner in the colonial dining room looking out onto the hundred year old gardens, and I wondered about days gone by when the archeologists were there. I'd read they had large staffs of locals to attend them, so even though their daily work was taxing, they fell into the genteel lifestyle of the turn-of-the-century upper class when back at hacienda headquarters.

We strolled outside to look for our cottage. The hotel staff had lit torches—to both repel mosquitoes and to light the narrow paths. Fragrant night-blooming jasmine scented the humid Yucatan air as we found our little bungalow again.

"Tired," Paul said as he unlocked the door letting us into the room.

"Me, too, but I think I'll read for a while. I've got a couple books on the Maya and this seems like the perfect spot to read them. If nothing else, I'll imagine what it was like when all those famous archeologists were here."

I'd brought along Linda Schele and David Friedel's *Maya Cosmos: Three Thousand Years on the Shaman's Path,* and *The Maya* by Michael Coe. Both books were written by present-day Mayan explorer/archeologists. Not exactly light reading, but I was in the mood for a Maya bedtime story. I'd just seen a spectacular light show commemorating Mayan gods and rulers and now I was nestled into a cottage that had once been occupied by famous Mayan archeologists. As far as I was concerned, there was no better place on earth to read this stuff. Tomorrow we would be on our way back to the coast and the jungles of Quintana Roo. Home to *Casa Maya* with artwork in tow. But tonight . . . tonight we were in the heart of Maya land.

On the Road

Back on the *autopista* paid highway, heading to Puerto Morelos the next day, I snuggled into the front seat with pencil and paper in hand, letting Paul do the driving, while I made a list of all the books I wanted to read to keep up with my blossoming Maya-mania. My early travels in Mexico had always been preceded by literary adventures, and my current pursuit of the Maya would follow the same path. My Mexico reading passion came in waves. First I read Carlos Castaneda's *Teachings of Don Juan: A Yaqui Way of Knowledge,* and became fascinated with Mexican mysticism. Then I stumbled onto B. Traven when I traveled the gringo trail in the '70s, starting with *The Treasure of the Sierra Madre,* his legendary tale about greed and gold in the mountains of Mexico. I continued reading Traven's Jungle Series detailing the hellish working conditions forced upon indigenous Mayans in the mahogany camps of southern Chiapas. My favorite of these was *Rebellion of the Hanged.*

I labored through D.H. Lawrence's *The Plumed Serpent,* read Graham Greene's *The Power and the Glory,* and digested Malcom Lowry's *Under the Volcano.* Carlos Fuentes' magical realism swept me away. For fun I romped through John D. MacDonald's Travis McGee novels, many taking place in Mexico.

Now I was onto Maya studies. Paul had noticed a new book-store at Chichen Itza when we left the sound and light show, and I'd picked up two famous Maya books, *Popol Vuh* and *Chilam*

Balam. *The Popol Vuh* was called the Mayan Bible, with fragments of Maya cosmology, mythology, and religion and the *Chilam Balam*, an ancient Maya text, had been written by a class of prophet priests or sooth-sayers, according to Sylvanus Morley. I also bought *Account of Matters in Yucatan,* by Diego de Landa, the priest whose religious zeal in 1553 prompted the burning of all but four Maya codices (paperbark books) relegating their history and culture to centuries of unsolved mysteries.

My new reading list included *Forest of Kings*, by Linda Schele and David Freidel. *Breaking the Maya Code,* by Michael Coe and *The Last Lords of Palenque,* by Robert Bruce and Victor Perera.

While I daydreamed about the Maya, the Spanish conquest, and all things Mexican, Paul provided the driving, and in less than a couple hours we were back on the coast. The Yucatan seemed a world away from Puerto Morelos, and even though we'd had an enjoyable trip, I was glad to be back at the beach.

Our friend Matt passed by as we pulled into the driveway and offered to help us unload our Mayan artwork from the car. Over cold Coronas in our new back yard we discussed where we'd place the Maya *stellae.* Matt was as fascinated as we were with Alfonso's artwork, and when we told him where the *stellae* look-alike was from, Yaxchilan, in Chiapas, he nodded his head in recognition.

"I thought it looked familiar," Matt said. "Do you want to hear one weird story about Yaxchilan?"

"Sure," I replied. I was always game for pyramid stories. "Can I get you another *cerveza* first? Paul?"

Two heads gave me the go-ahead, and I hurried inside the house to get two cold beers before I settled in for a true-to-life Mayan tale.

The only way to see Yaxchilan, our friend explained, was by long boat on the Usumacinta River, the river dividing Mexico and Guatemala. Since the site was impressive, the guide suggested a two day trip with an overnight in the jungle. Although they left early, the ancient truck taking Matt and his guide to the meeting spot down a washboard dirt road south of Palenque broke down. By sheer luck, another vehicle passed them and helped the driver patch the truck together for a quick repair. They drove onward to the river where they would meet up with a river guide who would take them by boat to Yaxchilan that afternoon.

Once on the river, Matt recounted, high rainforest on either side was alive with howler monkeys and tropical birds. It was like being in a dream. Until the outboard motor gave out. He couldn't believe his luck—two breakdowns the same day—one by land, one by sea. After several false starts on the outboard, both guides decided to give it a rest and try later. In five minutes, they were napping, while our friend simply sat in the long boat in the river, waiting. A half hour later, the guides woke up and began a new attempt at the motor. This time their patience was rewarded when the motor started immediately. Getting to Yaxchilan had become a full day's project. By the time they reached the site it was dusk, and they decided it was best to have supper and camp for the night. An odd assortment of other campers had chosen to do the same, and tents were pitched all along the banks of the river.

Over dinner, the guide told Matt stories about Yaxchilan, explaining it was a city of seers, where the bloodletting ritual took place (Mayan rulers would pierce themselves with sharp bones or obsidian blade fragments, collecting blood as an offering to the gods) so that the rulers could have visions of the future.

As night fell, Matt unrolled his sleeping bag and tried to get settled, in spite of jungle sounds and the eeriness of camping out in a rainforest. That night, he dreamt of the pyramids at

Yaxchilan. In his dream he walked through a labyrinth, and then walked from structure to structure, seeing *stellae* with women rulers, *stellae* with kings partaking in the ritual ball game. Then he dreamt he was in a huge ceremonial center with many intricately carved *stellae*.

In the morning he was quick to tell the guides his dream. They looked at him oddly, and went about cleaning up the campsite. Soon they were ready to hike into Yaxchilan. Imagine our friend's surprise when he approached the labyrinth, and it was exactly as in his dream. As he walked, now fully awake, he felt he was reliving his dream. He knew exactly what he would see next, what to expect. He had dreamed his tour of the site, and now he was walking through a waking dream, from building to building.

Paul and I were spellbound by his story. "That's incredible," I gushed. "I want to go to Yaxchilan."

"It's pretty dangerous to go there now," Matt cautioned. "I heard bandits came through the campsite a few months ago, where the trail begins. More than a dozen, carrying AK-47s. They demanded money and jewelry from the tourists, but no one was hurt. It's not safe."

The Palenque road south to Ocosingo and San Cristobal de las Casas was probably the most unsettled area in all of Mexico. The Chiapas Incident in 1994 took place in San Cristobal, and Ocosingo, just twenty miles south of Palenque, was known to harbor Zapatista rebels. *Federales* patrolled the area regularly. Maybe we'd save that trip for another time.

———————

Before we left for the States later that week, we planned to meet with Joe Marino and have a base made for our new *stellae*, then position it in the yard. We also planned to build a small koi pond. As time went on, we collected more Mayan artwork to be displayed on the grounds of *Casa Maya*, and we added colored Malibu lights for effect. Eventually the koi pond had a fountain with a statue of the head of Pacal. We built a small cement bench nearby so we could sit and watch the fish. We planted hundreds of coco palms over the years, both the local species, known only as "cocos" and the disease resistant *Malay* cocos, a palm from Malaysia that could withstand the lethal yellow rot that had killed off all coconut palms on the Quintana Roo coast starting in the early '90s. The disease had spread to Mexico from Florida, and the coco palms were almost universally wiped out because of it.

When Joe Marino came over to measure the *stellae* for the base, we asked him the logistics of moving our things, including my growing library of books, from San Francisco to Puerto Morelos.

"Just ship everything down and see what happens. Don't bother to provide paperwork. They'll work something out with you; it's done all the time," he assured me.

"But Joe, I have five thousand books. I'm an avid reader, and who knows, some day I just might open a bookstore in Mexico."

"A bookstore? You gotta be kidding. No one reads here," he insisted.

"Well, I do. And so do lots of other people. I'm constantly bringing suitcases filled with books for everyone I know. But what about the information we're supposed to have when we ship things down here. Like receipts, manifests, stuff like that?" I asked. "The Mexican Consulate says we need that to qualify for a one-time exemption from paying customs tax, if you're planning to make Mexico your permanent residence."

"You worry too much! Just pack up everything! For shipping

you'll have to use Hybur Trade in Miami. Since the Chiapas Incident in '94 all other U.S. shipping companies pulled out of Mexico. Nothing like a little revolution to shake up corporate America."

"I'll check with Hybur, then I have to line up a cross-country freight lines. Books are heavy. I know this won't be cheap. No one is crazy enough to ship all this weight."

"Only you!" Joe laughed.

"My reading habit is proving to be one expensive hobby! But at least I'll have lots of books for the beach!"

———⟫●⟪———

A week later we were back in San Francisco. The next eight months would crawl by. But this gave me time to collect even more books for my ever-growing collection, and to have three huge garage sales, to sell off everything we could of our furniture and household goods that we wouldn't need in Mexico.

We couldn't wait to move to our little fishing village. Over the years, we'd started to count the quirks that made the place so charming, and there were many. For example, in our town, the postman was also the garbage man. I couldn't understand why I never received letters people sent to me in Mexico. Then one of our local friends asked if I was tipping the postman. Of course not! I didn't know you tipped the postman! Well, in Mexico you do. I assumed since I didn't tip him, he'd been throwing my letters into the garbage.

After I was properly indoctrinated, the postman would drop off letters right at the house. Many times if I had a package, the announcement to pick up the package would come the day after it was to be sent back to the U.S., if not acknowledged. Timing is everything. But, I reminded myself, we did not move to Mexico for the postal system.

Regular mail, on the average, took three to four weeks to arrive from the States, but with Christmas cards, I usually received them mid-March. Christmas mail delays don't just occur in the U.S., I discovered. A friend told us never to mail anything of worth through the Mexican mail system, either from the U.S. or from Mexico, as the postal workers would most likely confiscate it. This changed over the years, when Vicente Fox became president and instigated a no graft policy, but I'm still of the old school, and avoid sending or receiving packages through the Mexican mails.

Generally, if I had to mail a letter, I found someone going back to the U.S. and asked them to mail it from there, a far more efficient process.

One year when I returned to Puerto Morelos after visiting family in California, I went to the postman's house to collect any letters that may have arrived while I was away. Going there was always a treat, because I could usually count on something out of the ordinary; also, our postman was a colorful addition to Puerto Morelos. When not riding around town on his ancient bicycle with wire basket filled with letters and packages, he could be found at home where his dining room table served as postal headquarters.

He was a gem—a Mexican version of the postman in the Italian movie, *Il Postino*. This time, he'd been sick with lumbago and mail delivery, I discovered, was even more sporadic than usual. When I asked him if I had any mail, he pointed to four huge, plastic see-through bags stuffed to the brim behind the couch and easy chair.

"Those are letters?" I asked, in awe.

"*Si*," he replied with a little shrug of his shoulders. Did I want to go through the bundles and look for any letters addressed to me?

I went through all the bags and found three letters for me plus a couple letters for friends, which I asked if I could take and deliver. Soon after that, we got a post office box in Cancun.

But these were the things we loved about Mexico, the fact that living there was different from the U.S. Life was slower, not so much pressure was put on the ordinary.

I even discovered that *"mañana,"* the word for "tomorrow" in text book Spanish, doesn't even really mean tomorrow, as in, the plumber will be here *"mañana."* As a friend explained, it simply means not today.

I busied myself with reading more about the Maya, doing as much research as I could, and seeking out any information I could find. I also became interested in the flora and fauna of tropical rainforests. The University of Oklahoma Press was a fantastic source on all things Mexican, Aztec and Mayan. I signed up for their quarterly book announcements and continued collecting in this area of interest. In the meantime, we lived and breathed Mexico.

After some discussion on shipping our books and personal items, we decided to go with Joe's assertion that little would be needed by Mexican customs to clear 5,000 books for my personal library from San Francisco to Puerto Morelos. After lining up a freight company we loaded all the boxes on a rented truck to take the books to Fremont where the shipping company was located. They were loaded onto a commercial truck, and my books were on their way.

Soon we were counting the weeks until we could leave San Francisco and drive with our kitten, Max, to Quintana Roo. After a flurry of retirement parties, we said goodbye to family and friends, packed what was left of our earthly belongings into our 1997 Ford Escort station wagon, and headed south.

———⇒⊷◄———

Once in Brownsville, Texas, we should have been able to loosen up, but we'd heard so many horror stories about this particular border town, we couldn't relax. After renting a hotel room and moving most of our luggage inside, we went out for dinner. On our arrival back at the hotel, we noticed a group of shady-looking guys hanging around two parked cars at the far end of the parking lot—we figured either for drug deals or illegal alien crossings.

The next morning we were up at 4 a.m. so we could arrive early at *la frontera,* the border. This was the best way to do it. We crossed with little hassle. Soon the sun was peeking at us from far distant mountains in the East, and we were driving towards our new Mexican home. For the first hundred miles, we saw little but Joshua trees on a flat, lifeless landscape. Occasionally we would pass an overloaded big rig, but other than that, very little traffic.

Tuxpan was our first stop, a city of 100,000, on a river. We'd driven twelve hours and had covered no more than five hundred miles. Mexican roads lived up to their reputation. Many had serious ruts and had to be driven at slow speeds. We had brought an extra tire with us, just in case we got a flat in the middle of nowhere.

The next night we stayed at Catemaco, just past Veracruz, on the gulf. Catemaco was known for its witches' festival each spring equinox. The city, tucked into the mountains in the heart of tobacco growing country, was situated on a lake. It was a pretty spot, but from the reaction of the townspeople, they hadn't seen many foreigners. I felt like an oddity. I was approached by a *bruja*, witch, who promised me she was a good witch and would help me.

Why me? I thought as I looked at this diminutive sorceress who wanted to alter my life. I just quit my corporate job after fifteen years, I built a dream house in the Yucatan, and now I was going there to relax on the beach. Life is good right now. Why did she have to come up to *me*?

I tried to dissuade her from helping me out with her charms. I wanted no flotsam and jetsam corroding my future. I didn't need a reading, a spell, nor a potion.

I gave a big smile, pretended I couldn't understand her, and started walking across the town square at a rapid gait with Paul at my side. I'd save the sorcery for another time.

Back on the road we pushed on towards the Yucatan. Past Villahermosa, we came upon the one town everyone told us to avoid, Escarcega.

"No matter what," Joe Marino had implored, "do *not* stop in Escarcega. They will rip you off. Escarcega is notorious."

Unfortunately, we needed fuel, and right after Escarcega there was a lonely two hundred mile stretch of road before we'd arrive in Chetumal. Glumly, we pulled into an extremely large Pemex gas station, with lots of trucks and big rigs and fifteen gas pumps. I climbed out of the car. One of us always stood outside and watched the pump while we were getting gas, to make sure we got what we paid for. Paul got out on the other side.

"*Señora*," I heard someone say. I turned around, and about knee-height I gazed down at a shabbily-dressed young man of eighteen with no legs, sitting on a low four-wheeled scooter, begging. He held his hand out, a pitiful gesture, just as a child of six ran up to me, bumping the lame boy's scooter, shouting "Chicklets, chicklets." Still trying to watch the gas gauge, I rummaged in my coin purse and found a couple pesos, gingerly dropping them in the lame boy's hand, and shushing the chicklet boy with a *"No gracias."*

Coming up on my other side was a smallish woman carrying a tin tray of sweets. Flies buzzed lazily over the wax paper carelessly wrapped around sugary dough balls, and before she cornered me between the chicklet boy and the car, I warded her off with a stern tone, *"No gracias, señora.* Paul, how's it going over there?"

Paul was busy fending for himself in this bizarre Mexican Fellini moment. The gas pump had just clicked off, and I saw him grab his wallet and narrowly open it while the pump attendant watched closely, hoping to get a display of what was inside. Paul pulled out two bills—one hundred peso note and twenty peso note. Very good, I thought, as I checked the pump. Total—one hundred and fifteen pesos. We always tried to give exact amounts rather than large bills at gas stations to inhibit short changing. That tactic seemed to keep everyone honest.

"Ready?" he asked, a slight grimace on his face.

"Yep," I replied, wondering what expression I wore after enduring this three-ring circus. I climbed back inside the safety of the station wagon. Now the chicklet boy was in front of the car, talking to the pump attendant. When Paul started the engine, he lept aside. "Well, that was a bad movie. It couldn't have been any weirder. No wonder Joe Marino told us to avoid Escarcega. I could have done without that."

In years to come Escarcega got such bad word of mouth from tourists, everyone would fill up with gas in Villahermosa, and drive on fumes to Chetumal. No one stopped in Escarcega. Mexico travel guides wrote warnings to tourists to count their change at the gas station, and to stop only in an emergency. It was an all points alert. Everyone avoided Escarcega. Years later, while driving through that dingy, dusty pit stop of a town, we noticed a newly painted sign hanging over a small wood frame bodega. *"Bienvenidos,* Welcome Tourists." The little wooden shack was, of all things, a tourist center. On seeing it, Paul and I laughed. For Escarcega, it was a case of too little, and way too late.

Just outside Escarcega the road narrowed and pastures popped up on either side. I settled into the drive, knowing we had a long way to go to Chetumal. This would be a day of driving. We'd decided, however, if we got to a stretch of little known pyramids at the halfway point, we'd take a short break, maybe have a sandwich from the cooler, and let our kitten, Max, walk around. I'd recently read about these pyramids in *National Geographic*—Kohunlich, Becan, Chicanna, and Xpuyil, near the great ceremonial center, Calakmul. These were smaller sites. Kohunlich, known for its Temple of the Masks, became famous in 1971 when looters tried to sell one of the site's huge stucco masks to New York's Metropolitan Museum of Art.

We made good time, seeing virtually no other cars on the road. Around 4 p.m. we neared Chicanna, and passed it. Then I saw the tower of Xpuyil from the road.

"Paul, can we stop?" I asked. I needed a break plus I really wanted to see one of these lesser known sites, void of the tourists and the hoopla. He nodded his head, and we pulled down a *sascab* lane a good ways past an open wire gate, into a rough parking area. I slowly got out of the car, while Paul saw to Max. I stretched, then went around to the trunk to find the cooler. I'd bought bread, mayonnaise and a couple cans of tuna fish. A quick sandwich would be welcome, as we'd just had fruit and juice for a late breakfast around 11 a.m., not wanting to take time to stop. I pulled out a plastic container for mixing, found the can opener, mayonnaise and bread, and started to put together a rather unglamorous tuna sandwich. As I was finishing up spreading the lumpy fish onto Bimbo wheat bread, I called to Paul. He'd put Max back inside, and we both leaned against the car, ready for our afternoon snack. After my sandwich, I told him I wanted to check out the site and have a look around. Just as I bit into the tuna fish, a white, older model International with a large tarp-covered trailer pulled into the parking area. Two men were in the truck, an older fellow was driving. The vehicle was about one hundred feet away from us when the guy riding shot gun jumped out. He was young, nineteen or so, lanky, and moved fast across the parking lot. The truck had Canadian plates, and the driver kept it idling.

"Weird, " I said to Paul. "I wonder what they're up to. Why did just one guy get out of the truck, and why isn't the driver turning off the motor?"

"That is weird," Paul agreed, as we saw the young man dart through the fence and run along the path leading to the pyramid.

With the truck still idling, we now watched this scene warily. "I don't feel good about this, Paul."

"Neither do I. What are they doing?" he asked, as he began to push things back into the trunk of the car. I followed his lead and closed the cooler, holding my sandwich in one hand, as I stuffed the can opener and bag of bread into the car.

"Let's get out of here. Something isn't right. Maybe they're scouting out the ruins for artifacts. What's the trailer for?" I asked.

"No, this isn't good," Paul agreed. "And why the tarp? The cat's inside, let's get out of here."

The truck had parked at just the right angle so we couldn't see the driver, as if it was planned that way. If these guys *were* looters, we didn't want to be around when INAH (National Institute of Anthropology and History) discovered them, or worse, the *federales*. Paul started the car, and headed towards the long driveway that led out to the highway. The white International was still idling when I turned around and gave it one last look.

"Grave robbers? Were they grave robbers?" I asked. "Or looters?"

"We don't want to know," Paul answered as we headed towards Chetumal, not waiting to find out.

We arrived at Chetumal, capitol of Quintana Roo, at 7 p.m. We'd covered a lot of miles that day, and knew we were close to home, but our rule was to never drive in Mexico at night. We checked into *Los Cocos*, one of Chetumal's nicer hotels, had dinner at their restaurant and were back in our room by 9 p.m. Time for sleep. Just as we began our descent into dreamland, we heard a ruckus in the hallway outside our door. Then someone flung open the door to the room next to ours, and God forbid, it sounded like the hallway crowd was piling into the hotel room, just a paper thin wall away.

Oh, no. What could be worse than partying Mexicans in the hotel room next door? Partying Mexicans in a border town known for drugs and money laundering in the hotel room next door. Disco music began to blare from a ghetto blaster, accompanied by a round of applause. I dared not knock on their door and ask if they could keep it down. And screaming "*Silencio!*" was out of the question. After all, I wanted to wake up the next morning.

Around 9:30 we were in for another treat. The *muchachas*, the girls, arrived. Now, along with the boom-boom of the music, an occasional high pitched squeal could be heard, then intense giggling and the infrequent scream.

By 1 a.m. things were leveling off. The music died down and I heard someone fall against the door, then I heard it open and a litany of good byes were uttered in Spanish. The girls were leaving. Thank God, *ojala!*

We were out of the hotel the next morning by 7 a.m. Four

hours later we arrived in Puerto Morelos. We'd take on customs later that week to retrieve our stuff and my books. For the balance of that day, our first as full-time Mexican residents, we were off the clock. We were, as they say, on Mexican time.

Mexican Shuffle

"Do you know any customs brokers?" I asked Joe Marino. "We need to get our things out of hock, and the consolidator in Miami said the shipment would be here any day now. What's the procedure?"

"I have a friend in Cancun who works as a customs broker. Let me call him and set up an appointment for you."

Thus began our customs saga—the one with us having no paper work, no receipts, *nada*. Nothing except lots of personal belongings and tons of books.

We met Joe's friend the next day in Cancun. His cramped office was packed with desks, tall file cabinets, ringing telephones, two secretaries. He was extremely busy, appeared to be high strung, and managed to ignore us in an office that was miniscule.

Antonio was thin and well-bred, an aristocratic Mexican, in the same class as our flamboyant attorney, Reynoldo Garcia, but apparently worlds apart in his view of gringos. He had a narrow face and longish nose; his accent oozed Spanish heritage. I felt we were decimated to the class of peons in his Castilian mind, and because we were gringos, I thought he'd rather step on us than assist us.

"Where is your manifest?" he demanded in sharp, staccato tones, each word stressed as though blasted from a trumpet. We'd barely announced who we were.

"We don't actually have a manifest," I countered, now wondering if Joe Marino could have given us better advice about customs' procedures. "What would it entail? A manifest?"

"You don't know," and he stressed the vowel in know, "what a manifest *is*?"

I jumped when he finished his question, he said it with such force. I was rattled.

"Um, no. Sorry . . ."

At this admission, he rose from behind his crammed-with-paperwork desk and started stabbing his pen at me in sharp, syncopated movements. "This, of course, is a *problem!*" he shouted, dramatically waving his arms high in the air.

I didn't know if not having a manifest was the problem, or my inability to identify one was the problem. But there obviously *was* one. I was glad of the desk's position between us. Paul looked at him as if he were from another planet.

I decided on a new approach. "What does a manifest do?" I asked, trying to get a handle on how indelicate this situation really was.

"A manifest identifies all items you are bringing in!"

Oh, no. I began to see the big picture. The one where not only did we have 5,000 books held hostage in Mexico, but we'd also airfreighted an unbelievable amount of personal effects, including fax machine, computer, printer, telescope, CD player, kitchen and home items; all lacked paper work.

"So how do we rectify this situation?" I asked. Joe said anything was possible in Mexico. It was time to test that theory.

"You create a manifest for me, and you include receipts of all your goods!" Antonio nearly screamed. I wondered if he drank a lot of coffee, or if he was always this disagreeable.

"Receipts? Of all our things? Are you serious?"

"Do I look serious to you?" This registered about an eight on a ten-decibel level.

"Yes, you certainly do," I said, beginning to get a hold of myself. Who was this madman? "I can give you a list tomorrow, or this afternoon, if you like. It may take me a few days to get receipts on everything; I may have to call the U.S. and have things faxed."

He looked at me as if I were a flea on a scroungy dog. I never before met anyone like him, and frankly, no one talked to me like this. I was glad I wasn't Mayan right then. Or wait a minute, maybe gringo fell *below* Mayan in the pecking order. I had to think about that for a minute... later.

"Listen, I'll make up the *manifest* and bring it back in half an hour. *Ciao*," I said, with conviction. When I spoke, he took on the look of a wild stallion, rearing, with thrashing hooves.

Paul and I stood in unison and marched out of his cramped, suffocating office. Now *we* were in a huff.

"Of all the priggish, horrendous jackasses I've met, he takes the cake! Of all the nerve! Who does he think he is? I thought *Alejandro* had an attitude."

"Maybe he doesn't want any new business," Paul smirked in an effort to make me laugh.

I burst out laughing. Antonio certainly hadn't put on his at-your-service hat before we stepped through the door. He wouldn't win any customer service awards. Paul and I share the same sense of humor, and use it to relieve tension, whenever necessary. Tension was high.

"I'll make up that stupid manifest and get it right back to him. I think I saw a coffee shop nearby. There it is, *Bisquettes*. Maybe a little caffeine will help me think. Man, I just hope I can remember all the stuff we packed."

For the next half hour, we sat at the coffee shop drinking coffee and racking our brains to come up with a working list of all the worldly belongings we'd (foolishly?) shipped to Mexico, both by airfreight and by container.

"What should we put for books, Paul? I think we're allowed to bring in one hundred."

"They *are* for your personal library, all 5,000. You better put the full amount, in case they decide to open boxes and count them."

"Oh, boy. Okay, I guess I have no other choice," I glumly noted.

Ready for round two, in a caffeine daze, we headed back towards Antonio's office. At least we would meet him on common ground, strung out and wired.

As we entered, one of the secretaries gave me a sympathetic look. I felt like I was going to a hanging. Mine.

"We have our list, Antonio," I stated, matter-of-factly, as he waved us into his overcrowded quarters. "I mean—*manifest*." I gave him a prim little smile.

"Is this for personal use or commercial use?" he demanded.

"Personal," Paul and I answered in unison.

"Well, then," he said, pausing dramatically, "why do you have a *stapler* on this manifest?" He practically spat out the word.

"I use staplers all the time. Everyone does, in the States."

"No they don't! Staplers are for offices! This is a commercial list!"

"Really, it's not! I like to have a stapler around my office . . . ."

"Your office! See!" he gave me a threatening look.

"No, no. I mean my *home* office. Everyone in the U.S. has home offices. Really they do."

"This will never work. Customs will demand a commercial invoice."

Oh, man. I could hardly wait until he saw those 5,000 books for my personal library.

"Isn't there some way we can work this out? I mean, if we

have to pay something, we understand," I said.

"Are you insinuating that Mexican officials take bribes? In customs? " he questioned, posing this as a threat.

"Certainly not! What a silly notion!" I was backpedaling at high speed now. "I simply meant, if there was more paperwork you needed to complete to *assist* us, then of course, we'd be more than willing to pay for it."

That said, he looked further down the list and onto the second page. I saw him take in a sharp breath and hold it. For way too long.

"What is this?" he asked as he began drumming his fingers rapidly on the cluttered mahogany desk. Even the cheesy offices here had hardwood furniture, I couldn't help noticing.

I assumed he'd found the list of books.

"Can I see what you're looking at?" I said in a conciliatory gesture, leaning over to see the paper he held.

"Five thousand books! Is that a mistake?" Antonio, the inquisitor, asked.

"Well, no. You see, I like to read and . . . ."

"This will never, never, *never* go through! Ever! Where are your documents?"

I was Ingrid Bergman in *Casa Blanca* being grilled by Claude Rains.

"Documents . . . well, Joe Marino told us we could get them this week if everything went smoothly and wasn't too much of a problem, but I see maybe he was mistaken about *that* . . . How about if we leave this with you," I motioned at the manifest I'd just created, "and we'll call you when we have more information ready. But now, *I* have a question for you. Isn't this what you do? Get people's things out of customs?"

"Of course!"

"Well, try that for us, and we'll get back to you later this week," I said, staring him straight in the eye as I moved away from the desk. "You can call Joe Marino if there's anything else you need from us. Thanks for your time."

End of round two, and the beginning of an administrative nightmare. Obviously post-NAFTA Mexico was changing, and we were caught in the net.

———⟶♦⟵———

My books, which had come in by cargo container, miraculously cleared customs within three weeks which amazed me after meeting the rudest bureaucrat I would ever encounter, Antonio, our customs broker. Remarkably, the books, which sat on the dock for most of that time, were easier to release than our household goods which came in by air.

Now came our next hurdle, immigration. When we'd last been in Cancun, before our move to Mexico, we'd been introduced to a notary who told us he'd assist with our paperwork when we wanted to get our FM3s, or green cards. An FM3 allowed a foreigner to reside in Mexico as a non-immigrant for a period of one year. The FM3 document needed renewal each year as long as one continued to reside in Mexico. To obtain an FM3, a current tourist visa was required, a passport, proof of income (for a retired status) of roughly $12,000 U.S. per year without owning a house in Mexico, and $6,000 U.S. per year if one owned a house in Mexico, and finally, a letter signed by two Mexican witnesses stating that one qualified as an upstanding person in the community. After these documents were received by immigration, a standard form had to be submitted along with photographs, passport copies, and a letter of authorization.

It really didn't seem that difficult, but the immigration attorney we'd hired must have been brain dead. We'd actually inherited him from another notary who didn't know how to process immigration documents, and I was beginning to wonder if this second dolt was any more capable than the first. When we met the first notary, he'd requested obligatory gift items right up front—San Francisco Giants baseball cap, Nike sweatshirt, and Forty-Niners tee shirt—long before he lifted a finger towards processing our documents. That should have been a signal he'd be long gone by the time we needed his services. And he was.

We tried to reach him numerous times, and he simply was not returning calls. A friend told us we could process our own paperwork and turn it in to immigration. If only things were that simple. Again, like lambs to the slaughter, we innocently began another rite of passage—the immigration trap.

Our tourist visas were good for ninety days, and just before that timeline was up, we went to immigration to process paperwork for our FM3s. It was mid December, and as newcomers to Mexico, we had no clue that every government office in the country closed for a three week holiday from mid December until after New Year's. We waded through the procedures, blissfully ignorant of the cutoff date. The clerk at the counter kept telling us to come back later. Finally, frustrated by our lack of progress, our countless trips to immigration, and the near expiration of our tourist passes, we asked our friend Alberto to go with us that Friday. We arrived at immigration with Alberto, pulled a number, and took a seat. I held my breath as our number was called. In the cold, sterile environment of the immigration offices, possibly filled with the world's worst vibes, I felt a kinship to those facing similar treatment in the U.S. Now I knew, first-hand, the displacement one feels as a stranger in a strange land.

Alberto went up to the counter with us as we awaited the fate of our immigration status. He spoke quietly to the female clerk as she motioned her finger to wait a moment. Into the bowels of government she went, to the chief administrator, the *jefe*. When she was gone a good five minutes, I started to feel faint. The clerk returned, gave a little shake of her head, then stared at me as she handed the letter my way. I passed it to Alberto, as it was written, of course, in Spanish, and he could peruse it quickly. It looked very formal and highly suspicious. In a moment he looked up from the document and spoke in Spanish to the clerk, who had continued to stand at the counter across from us.

Again she shook her head, this time a bit haughtily, and responded in Spanish, but her reply was low and fast, and I couldn't catch it. I gazed at the letter over Alberto's elbow, and saw a negative check by status.

"Alberto, does this mean we won't get our FM3s?" I asked, pointing at the derisive check mark.

"Well, not right now, but they will give you an extension."

"Turn the page," I commanded, now seriously nervous. We were nearing the last days of the government work year. We were close to an immigration deadline. "Please read it to me, what does that say?"

"It says you have failed to complete all necessary forms by the proper dates, and because of this, you will need to return on a visitor's pass, and start the procedure from the beginning."

"What? Oh no! I can't believe it!"

"Let's go outside," Alberto instructed, "out of these offices, so we can talk."

He herded us past the countless other peons who waited, innocent as sheep, for their FM3s. I saw no one, nothing but a blur, as we moved out the door into the harsh sunlight.

"What does the letter say, exactly?" I demanded, still feeling faint.

"It says you have fifteen days to leave the country."

"What?" Paul and I both shrieked in unison. "Leave the country?"

"I'm afraid so," Albert said, looking upset. "We need to find you an immigration attorney."

"We need to find a hit man," I countered, "for that immigration clerk who kept telling me to come back later."

"Now what do we do?" Paul asked.

"We have to find someone fast. Any ideas, Alberto?"

"Jeanine, don't worry. I will find a lawyer for you," Alberto said in as soothing a voice as possible. "We will work this out. You know how it is here; if you have money, all can be made right."

Magically Alberto was as good as his word and produced an immigration attorney who made time for us that very afternoon. When we met Claudia we were surprised at her youth, but her persistence and knowledge of immigration law seemed firmly in place.

"You will need to leave as soon as possible, either to the States or to Belize," she instructed as we sat in her glass-enclosed conference room, clearly in shock.

"We'll go to Belize, whenever you suggest," I replied in a despondent manner.

"The sooner, the better," she said, "since this is December and immigration closes for the holidays soon. If you don't get the paperwork processed this year, you will pay a huge fine for continuation into a new year."

"Oh, God. I can't believe this," I muttered.

"Please do not worry," Claudia implored in the kindest manner. "This is really not so bad."

"Claudia, to us this is bad. They want us to leave the country; we're being *instructed* to leave the country!"

"We can work this out quickly, I am sure. And I think it can be done before the holidays. My father knows someone in immigration."

The Mexican way, either you paid through the nose or you were connected.

"Well, we can leave today," I said looking at Paul for confirmation.

"Yes," he said, "we should probably get down to Belize and back as soon as we can. It's 3 p.m. now; we can make it by sunset."

"Really?" Claudia responded, apparently impressed by our ability to make snap decisions. "That would be very good, because then, you will be back by Tuesday. You will have to stay three days in Belize before you can return. I can meet with you Tuesday afternoon and by then, I will have met with the *jefe* at immigration." She smoothed back her long, brown hair that had been tied in ponytail fashion with an elegant, blue velvet ribbon. Her starched, long-sleeved blouse was tucked snugly into business-like slacks, navy blue. Her outfit was set off with a smart, satin cummerbund that was wrapped tightly around her narrow waist.

"Why didn't they just process our paperwork?" I asked.

"Sometimes, immigration goes through departmental changes and the status of some documents can be misplaced. Or at other times, there are slow ups in processing immigration papers to certain nationalities because of different political situations. Like Proposition 187 in California."

"You mean the California illegal alien proposition that was recently defeated? Not allowing immigrants health and education benefits? " I asked, amazed by this realization. "So we're experiencing a backlash?"

"I'm not saying that for sure, but at times reprisals occur. Mexico is very aware of what happens in the States with immigration, because so many people from this country migrate there, either legally or otherwise. But do not worry, Juanita, I will help you. Please be confident. Go to Belize."

Within fifteen minutes we were on our way, stopping quickly at the house to pick up a change of clothing. We were heading south again, but this time, it was unexpected—a detour to Belize.

Borderline Belize

Night had fallen as we pulled into the federal customs area at the border dividing Mexico and Belize. What is it about night border crossings that scares the bejesus out of me? I wondered as I gazed at a uniformed *federal* armed with M-16. His outpost, dark and securely locked, looked like a third world Checkpoint Charlie, a scene out of a '50s film noir.

"*No pasa,*" he explained, when I rolled down the car window to ask for instructions.

"I guess we can't take the car through until we speak to someone inside, " I told Paul.

We moved the car closer to the garrison and stopped. In what would be the first of several bad decisions, we left the car parked in the federal zone. That night we simply weren't thinking. We were frazzled, bewildered, rebuffed . . . and scared. Never before had we been at a border crossing without a tourist visa. Now all we had was a letter from Mexican immigration asking us to leave the country. Who wouldn't be scared? We had no idea how the border patrol would digest that bit of information. Obviously immigration viewed us as wayward types. What would the border police think?

"Let's go ask and see what they want us to do."

We crossed the pit-holed, two lane road and walked with trepidation towards the Mexican immigration offices. We needed to start there to receive an exit visa from Mexico before crossing into Belize.

Near the entryway of the non-descript government building, we passed two men in uniform, smoking cigarettes. I could feel their eyes on me as they sized us up. At borders, I'd learned to avoid eye contact with anyone; it simplified things.

On entering the fluorescent brightness of the customs area, a man in a brown government uniform asked in Spanish how he could assist us.

I explained we had a letter from immigration for him, detailing our predicament. We planned to cross over to Belize for three days, then come back to Mexico, our adopted home land, where we now lived and owned a house.

As I explained our plight, one of the men we'd seen smoking on the front porch came to listen. Then a discussion began between these two men as to how our situation should be handled. Within a few minutes, it was obvious that Colonel Hernandez, one of the smokers from the porch, was the man in charge. *El jefe.*

"Do you have a vehicle?" he asked in Spanish.

I assured him I did.

"Where is it parked?"

I pointed to our car; it was just within sight, parked by the *aduana* (customs) station.

"Actually, I need to clear the car before crossing the border," I told him.

"Too late. They close at 3 p.m.," he replied curtly. "Let me see your papers. These are fine. You can cross now. I'll stamp them," he continued as he stretched out his hand towards one of the clerical workers, who instantly grabbed a rubber date stamp and handed it to the *jefe.*

Bam-bam! Bam-bam! And we were legal again—ready to depart Mexico.

"Just leave now, cross over, and return this evening," Colonel

Hernandez commanded, as he handed me the newly stamped documents. The ink was still wet.

"But I thought we had to spend three days in Belize?"

"It's just as easy to do it this way. You live in Mexico and you own a home here. I understand your situation and will approve this. Just cross the border now. You will be back in fifteen minutes."

"Are you sure it's okay?" I asked, as a small knot began forming in the pit of my stomach.

"Of course," he nodded, his eyes never leaving mine. "I am in charge."

No doubt about that.

Paul and I exchanged glances. We both wondered about the car, but here was Colonel Hernandez telling us all was fine. He had stamped our papers, our exit visas. We were ready to roll.

"*Gracias. Hasta luego,*" I said without conviction as we walked out into the now nearly pitch black night. The razor wire on the bridge gleamed menacingly, and the other *aduana* watched us depart as we picked up our pace while heading for the bridge, the boundary between Mexico and Belize. What it actually crossed over, I was not sure, so black was the night. I assumed it was a river.

Once the immigration office was out of sight, I started to panic. "Paul, what about the car? Is it okay?"

"I don't know. Did that look like a "no parking" area?"

"God, I'm not sure. I think we better hurry!" I urged, as we started trotting towards Belize. We could see the immigration offices from where we were, but the distance looked at least two hundred yards. In itself, the crossing was poorly lit, fraught with pot holes, ditches, the occasional rock, and a steady stream of other travelers who were slowly making their way through the darkness. Our fellow immigrants were Mexican, some black

Caribes, but not another gringo in the lot.

The closer we came to the Belize border, the more orderly it appeared, and their immigration offices looked newly remodeled and brightly lit.

I entered first, now in panic mode, tearing my passport from my purse, and whispering loudly to Paul, "Your passport!"

Behind a glassed-in enclosure sat an attractive black woman with fine, high cheekbones, skin the color of dark coffee beans, and hair neatly plaited in corn rows with bright beads worked in at the ends. To pass the time, she was paging carelessly through a fashion magazine. She looked up as we ran in; it was a slow night for border crossings—no one else was in line. In fact, the entire building was empty except for her, us, and a lifeless security guard at the door. On our entry, she straightened herself and watched us approach, putting the magazine on the counter beside her.

Full panic had hit, and like a derelict, I threw our passports on the desk in front of her. It finally occured to me: we were illegally parked on the Mexican side of the border, smack dab in the middle of a customs zone. If the Mexican authorities so desired, they could seize our car.

"What am I supposed to do with these?" she asked, an edginess to her voice.

"Can you stamp them, please? Mexican immigration said we could cross over tonight, and come back tomorrow with our car."

"Oh, so that's what Mexico told you? What do you think we are? Some trivial little country that you people can just use? You think you can run across the border," she had that part right, "and have us stamp your passports? Then scurry back to Mexico? Well, I got *news* for you, girl. You have to stay in our little, bitty country for three days before you'll get a thirty-day extension on your papers. Using us! Why don't you spend some of your tourist dollars here? We're sick of this—always back to Mexico they go."

At that point she started to shake her head and mumble, "People using us like this—sick of it." She was now moving her head from side to side, in rapper mode.

Talk about an attitude. I grabbed our passports from under the glass casing before her hands could touch them and Paul and I were running again, now towards the door, and then back to the Mexican border.

Once outside, almost out of breath, I gasped, "Paul, we're in no man's land. We don't have an exit stamp for departure. Maybe Mexico won't let us back in. And our car is illegally parked! What are we going to do?"

"Run as fast as you can!"

We dodged diminutive Mexican women hunched over with bundles, jogged around mothers pulling weary children by hand, tried to avoid deep ditches that dark, beleaguered night. We were indeed in limbo, some nether region that connects countries—the border zone.

Belize customs officials, all along the bridge, watched in wonder as—after just having viewed us run into their immigration offices, they now watched us run back out towards Mexico. They were no doubt wondering exactly what we were asking ourselves, "What's Mexico going to do?"

Breathless, we came running back into Mexican immigration no more than ten minutes since Colonel Hernandez had stamped our exit papers. He looked up in surprise from where he sat at his barren, government issue desk, as we stormed back into the office.

I hurriedly explained, as I tried to catch my breath, that Belize wouldn't stamp our passports unless we stayed there three days, and since our car was on the Mexican side, we thought we'd best take care of business tomorrow, all at once. And by the way, could we cancel out that exit stamp we just received and start fresh *mañana*?

Maybe we took the colonel by surprise, I'll never know, but he simply canceled out the exit visa he had just created for us, pounding the rubber stamped signature with a flourish onto yet another form and said, "*Hasta mañana*."

We ran to our Escort wagon, jumped in, and roared off to Chetumal, still not believing we weren't in jail in either Belize or Mexico for not having proper exit and entry papers. While driving, we decided on a plan. We'd rent a room at the *Los Cocos* Hotel in Chetumal for three nights. The room, which included space in the enclosed parking area, would actually be rented so we could safely leave our car somewhere on the Mexican side of the border. Strange as it seemed, we were renting a hotel room for our car. After the evening's drama, we thought it made more sense to venture across the border car-less. We could then spend our three obligatory days in Belize with fewer worries.

Next morning we were up early for our border crossing. We'd paid for three nights at the hotel, and arrived by cab at the border. When we entered the customs area, only one of the men from the previous night was working the morning shift. He looked very serious, acted a bit aloof, and made a game of ignoring us. I was scared to death.

After we walked up to the counter, he came over to the clerk who was assisting us and said, "Weren't you in Belize last night?"

"*Buenos dias.* Is Colonel Hernandez here?" I asked, pointedly ignoring the question. "He told us to come back this morning and he'd take care of everything."

"I saw you last night. Where is your stamp? From Belize?" he pressed.

"We never received one, because we actually didn't go into

the country," I began. "Colonel Hernandez said we could come back today."

"Wait a minute," the new *jefe* said, in a commanding tone. He crossed the room towards the back of the building where there were several doors, all closed. He opened one of them, and disappeared.

The five minutes he was gone were the longest five minutes in my life. The door in back finally opened, and the new *jefe* came out, then swaggered over to us. In any other circumstances, I probably would have viewed him as handsome, but in a deadly way—kind of Eric Estrada goes south of the border. But now, fear had taken over.

He came close to me at the counter and spoke in a quiet tone. "Colonel Hernandez says you live here in Mexico?"

"That's right," I answered, "we have a house here."

"What did that liar at Belize immigration tell you?" he demanded.

I was shocked by his use of the word liar for another customs agent, no matter what country they might be affiliated with, but I acted nonchalant.

"She told us we had to stay in Belize three days, or no papers."

"Well, I will prove that liar wrong. Colonel Hernandez told me to give you an extension for six months. *Feliz Navidad!* You belong in Mexico! And you did not have to go through that Godforsaken country, Belize! All we need is this!" he said, as he picked up the fundamental component of border patrols: a rubber stamp complete with an immigration official's smudged signature. Really, it came down to no more than that.

The new *jefe's* assistant, anticipating our good luck, was already re-writing our papers—this time tourist visas—what we were after.

Within ten minutes we were out of there and catching another cab, back to the hotel to check out—and then to liberate—our car. After retrieving it, we drove stealthily back to immigration, now to register the car with our new tourist visa information. In Mexico, tourist pass and vehicle certificate must correlate. Now the car was out of sync. It was still attached to our defunct tourist passes. So much red tape, so many ways to snare oneself in an immigration snafu. In Mexico, one thing we had already learned, your paperwork must be current.

On our arrival back at the border, we decided to park the car a couple blocks away from the zone of terror, to avoid any of the players involved in last night's activities, just for safety's sake. We didn't want any changes of heart.

We carefully picked an innocuous side street, next to a small cafe. Although I noticed a group of men eating breakfast, I thought nothing of it until one of them stood up and I recognized his government uniform. Sitting at a corner table were four immigration workers—the very men we were trying to avoid. We'd carefully parked our illegal vehicle directly in their sight-line. Planning is everything.

Although they also noticed us, they appeared unconcerned and far more interested in their breakfast than in chasing us down. We walked peacefully up the street to have our car registered for legal entry into Mexico on our freshly stamped tourist visas. Somehow we obtained papers for the car without even crossing into Belize.

Four hours later we were back in Puerto Morelos. We pulled the car into the driveway, locked the gate, went inside and collapsed. We didn't even leave the premises until Tuesday, when we had a date with our attorney.

Suffice it to say, Claudia performed her job efficiently and freed us from our immigration hell. Our other-worldly border adventure made visits to the Cancun immigration office seem tame in comparison. The unplanned trip to Belize had been a revelation. We'd experienced the real jungle of Mexico, and in it—there wasn't a tree, nor a bird, not an animal to be found. The true jungle was the convoluted system of loose justice dispensed at border crossings everywhere—no matter what land, what country, what continent you inhabited.

For the authorities who govern borders live by their own book of rules, in a world that they devise, and in a dominion all their own.

El Fin

We settled into our new life in the Yucatan, happily content in the change of pace from mid-stream America. We met our neighbors, went fishing and snorkeling, read books, and enjoyed weekend trips to Merida or Valladolid. We took our first year off—for travel and relaxation—before further contemplating the idea of a bookstore. I was happy knowing I had a huge collection of books to read and to lend, and most of all, I knew I would never ever run out of reading material. That year we got comfortable in Mexico and acclimated to our surroundings. First things first.

Occasionally when driving south towards Playa del Carmen, we noticed the land we almost owned with Alejandro and thought about what might have been.

Whatever became of Alejandro's grandiose project? For years, he tried to find more investors. Some came, some went. Shortly after *Casa Maya* was built, we contacted him and asked when it might be possible to recoup our costs. He told us serious development was still a long way off, but he'd recently landed a couple new investors and he could return our money for the lot we had tried to purchase. Within days a cashier's check arrived—no paperwork—since we'd never held title on the property. At last, the land deal with Alejandro was no longer unfinished business, but a fait accompli. We were reimbursed.

We called him to say thanks and he wished us luck in our venture and gave us an update on his large scale, eight hundred hectare project. Since the property was so enormous, he was constantly fighting development costs, he told us, so he was still looking for big time investors.

More years passed and Cancun continued to grow as a tourist metropolis. As the city gained a worldwide reputation, the Tulum Corridor (south of Cancun) was renamed the Riviera Maya, and all-inclusive resorts began to spring up, many of them Spanish-owned. Rumors began to circulate that some of the resorts were dynamiting limestone shelves in the Caribbean to create more bays and inlets. Environmental restrictions slowly began to emerge for the Riviera Maya; in retrospect, it was a matter of too little, too late. In 2001, Vicente Fox's Environmental and Natural Resources Minister Victor Lichtinger, said, "tourism has to be based on the projection of Mexico's beauty . . . environmental laws which have been used selectively or ignored, will now be enforced. In the past, not only here (Quintana Roo) but in all of Mexico, we've been very discretionary in the application of the law."

During former Governor Villanueva's reign, the damage had been done. Many of the mega-resorts played the game by submitting design and developmental plans to the planning commission with all the "I's" dotted and "T's" crossed. For instance, a two-story maximum height was considered the legal limit on oceanfront properties, so new resorts submitted two story structural drawings to the planning department. What they would build, however, would be three story hotels. Near Akumal, one hotel had been warned to stop filling in mangroves as the new environmental laws deemed this illegal. Rumor had it an official planned a visit to the site, to declare an end to the project. Two days before his arrival, bulldozers worked through the night, illuminating the way with mercury vapor lights, to land fill as much as possible before the official arrived and ordered a work stoppage.

With twenty-two thousand hotel rooms already in Cancun, the Riviera Maya tallied thirteen thousand rooms by 2001, with plans to double that figure by 2006. Lichtinger made a promise to "build *cabañas,* aimed at people who like to be surrounded by nature. We are not going to continue to build huge resorts (in the southern half of the Costa Maya)." Only time will tell.

On another drive to Playa del Carmen, we noticed Alejandro's frontage land had been cleared and an impressive landscaping job was underway. The next time we passed by we saw the finishing touches on a grandiose project—a sweeping entrance had been completed for an eco-park named Lost Rivers. Alejandro had pulled it off.

We drove into the wide driveway, parked the car, and walked to the entrance where we were greeted by a young Mayan who led us to an admissions *palapa.* We were very curious to know if Alejandro was involved in this new environmental park.

"What activities does Lost Rivers offer?" I asked as an opener.

"The park has three natural rivers, very unusual in the Yucatan. Our guests can kayak or canoe down the rivers to the ocean, where there's a *cenote.* If you don't want to row or kayak, we have bicycles and bike paths. The snorkeling is good, plus we have a nice beach and a good restaurant where you can have lunch. An all day pass is $20 U.S. This is an eco-park, so we've kept everything ecologically sound, in all natural surroundings. There are wild orchids and bromeliads in the park growing alongside the mangroves. It's a nature preserve."

"We know this land; we've been down one of the rivers, to the *cenote,*" Paul said. "We know the owner, or we assume he's still the owner. Alejandro?"

"Alejandro. Yes, he's leased the land for Lost Rivers to a group of investors for ninety-nine years. He wanted to build a hotel or condos down by the *cenote,* but now there are environmental restrictions. To create an infrastructure, he needed to fill mangroves and that's no longer legal. Mangroves are protected here by law. They work as a natural filter for the ocean and as a nursery for marine life. If the mangroves die, the coral reefs will start to deteriorate, as they feed off each other."

"Yes, we know. We live in Puerto Morelos," I interjected, "and we know how important it is to keep the mangroves healthy. The mangroves are protected by law in Puerto Morelos, too, at least for now."

"Thanks for the information," Paul said to the worker, "maybe we'll come back next week and use your park."

We waved good bye and started walking back to the parking lot.

"Well, it's a good thing we followed Plan B," I said as we neared the car. "Alejandro wouldn't have been able to build here after all. Too many environmental restrictions these days. It took him so long to get it together that the laws changed before he could activate his master plan."

"If we'd waited these last eight years for him to find investors, which he obviously has," Paul continued, "we'd have wasted our time. As it is, *Casa Maya* has been built now for almost a decade."

"You're right. What if we'd waited it out, only to discover the new laws restricted what could be built on the property?"

"Well, it all worked out for the best, for all of us. He returned our money for the land, that was fair enough. We gambled, he threw the dice. It was all just luck."

"But I do believe he was a visionary. He saw eco parks as the wave of the future. And he had sound environmental ideas. Even that day when we were cutting the trail with him, remember? He was telling us then he was going to keep this all as green as possible. He wanted to merge with nature, not destroy it—save the *cenote*, the rivers, do very little land fill."

"I'm glad something finally happened, and he's gotten his money back," Paul said. "I still think he was set back at the very beginning when he lost his original Playa del Carmen land by eminent domain to the Playa car ferry that never materialized. He sat on *this* property for a long, long time."

"I'd never have had the patience. Well, it worked out well for us. We built *Casa Maya* and we're right next to his property where we first set foot in Puerto Morelos all those many years ago. Who would ever believe this story? It sounds like a tale from the Yucatan.

We looked forward to Easter week when we'd planned to travel to Palenque. I'd fallen in love with pyramids, and after seeing Chichen Itza, Cobá, Tulum, Ek Balam—Palenque beckoned.

After reading *Forest of Kings*, by Linda Schele and David Freidel, Palenque took over my imagination. To Schele, this pyramid site topped the list of most sacred. The Lacandon Maya still lived there, supposedly the last link to the Maya hierarchy. During the conquest, Hernando Cortez' premise had been to destroy all lineage to rulers, priests, and aristocracy. As Robert Bruce wrote in *The Last Lords of Palenque*, "the great teachers and leaders were murdered, the books burned, the schools and temples razed . . . (leaving) the people confused, leaderless, and enslaved." Everywhere else but Chiapas, this annihilation occurred. But near Palenque, some Maya escaped to the forests, avoiding extermination. Approximately four hundred Lacandones live in Chiapas today, a direct link to the ancient rulers of Palenque. Today, other Maya sects total nearly eight million, occupying land in Yucatan and Chiapas in Mexico, and in Guatemala, Honduras, and Belize. As winter turned to spring and Easter arrived, we prepared for a journey back to the States to see family and friends. We drove south through Chetumal, the capitol of Quintana Roo, then veered west towards Escarcega. Within one hundred miles after turning inland away from the coast, an opaque haze appeared. This smoky residue accompanied us for close to a thousand miles of our journey. It was spring, and the Mayans had begun an age-old ritual: slash and burn agriculture. Bruce wrote, in *The Last Lords of Palenque*, that "the Lacandon jungle, one of the world's richest rain forests, grows on some of the world's poorest soil, most of which consists of a few inches of topsoil covered by a few more inches of extremely rich leaf mold. After the Maya cut trees and clear them away, they plant corn, beans, and squash. By the second year of cultivation, the soil is near exhaustion." In days gone by, they moved on and cleared more virgin jungle by slashing and burning, Bruce wrote, as there was still room to spare. But during the Mexican Revolution, "thousands upon thousands of homesteaders moved into the area to practice a subsistence economy based on slash-and-burn agriculture. Each family cleared an area of several thousand square meters, and burned a fortune in fine tropical hardwoods in the process."

Continuing to this day, Mayans burn off their maze fields so they can plant anew. Road signs request that no fires be lit, but cultural habits apparently die hard, as we observed small fires for miles as we drove.

On arriving in Palenque, we chose Hotel *Chan-Ka*, a group of cottages on the Chacamax River. The cottages were made of river rocks, a soft gray in color and beautifully smooth after who knew how many millennium of repetitiously being washed by water. Flora reminiscent of Hawaii's tropics abounded. A dense, verdant green of heliconia, red and pink ginger, and birds-of-paradise made up the hotel's exterior gardens. I felt a sense of peace come over me as we unpacked the car and brought our belongings to the expansive porch of our cabin. Huge limbs of ancient trees held up the roof; small river rocks were cemented into the floor design; simple yet naturally elegant.

Our cabin sat directly on the river. As Paul unlocked the mahogany door, a light rain began to fall, a momentary phenomenon for April. I felt washed clean after driving through the smoky haze we'd experienced along the highway during the day.

After quickly unpacking, we left for the pyramid site. It closed at sunset and we still had an hour of daylight. The drive was short as we were only two kilometers away. The road hugged the river, and giant trees, species I'd not seen before, were scattered in the adjacent fields. At one time this had all been dense forest, but as tropical hardwoods became scarce, the larger trees had been cut and sold. Still, a few graced Palenque's perimeter and I surveyed them as we passed by. Slowly we ascended the road to the pyramid site.

On arrival, I was a bit stunned by the atmosphere at the site. It was quite unlike anything I'd seen at the pyramids in the northern Yucatan. Here at Palenque, the Lacandones retained free range of the area, and the result was carnival-like in setting. Inside and outside the entryway and spreading into the parking area, indigenous Mayans' blankets covered the ground, displaying bright shirts and shorts, colorful arrows, wooden plaques, stone carvings. The musky smell of copal, a Maya incense, burned everywhere, leaving a light cloudy haze in its wake.

The Lacadones themselves were the most beautiful native people I'd yet seen in Mexico: their skin was smooth, taut and tan in color. They had high cheekbones, dark, brilliant eyes, and they emitted an aura I can barely describe.

To me, it felt like they were not there in spirit. Their bodies existed, their molecules took up space, but it was as if they had dreamed these bodies and I was sleepwalking in *their* dream. They completely disregarded my existence. It was an eerie feeling, but it did not make me feel uncomfortable. They also emanated a feeling of sadness. Bruce, too, in *The Last Lords of Palenque,* found it a challenge to describe the Lacandones. He called their watchfulness, from a cool and proper distance, "poised, stemming from the desire to find their correct place in the universe, in order to live in the greatest possible peace and harmony. This came out in a total ease in their appearance and also in their language."

Inside the site, the first view I had was of a stand of massive *Ceiba* trees, the Maya tree of life. The trees put out purple flowers, then seed pods with white, fluffy cotton. I'd never seen a tree like this in bloom before, and it was stately, with large, straight limbs extending out, as if it could hold up the world. From this view, surrounded by *Ceibas,* I looked straight up at the Temple of Inscriptions. Directly across from it stood the Palace, with a three story tower, Asian in style. In the background, I heard what sounded like lions roaring.

"Paul, do you hear that noise?"

"Howler monkeys," he replied. "In the tall trees beyond the Temple of Inscriptions."

I looked up at the forest of thousand year old trees behind the pyramid that housed Pacal's tomb, listened attentively to the barking roar of monkeys in the background, felt the damp humidity of Chiapas as it engulfed my very being, and I realized this mysterious land of contrasts—pyramids, beaches, jungles, and colonial cities—now lived in me.

Bibliography

The following books and articles were helpful as resource material:

Coe, Michael D. *Breaking the Maya Code*. New York: Thames and Hudson, 1993.

Coe, Michael D. *The Maya, Sixth Edition*. New York: Thames and Hudson, 1999.

Corzo, Cynthia, Curtis Morgan and John Barry. "A Cornered Ship, 31 Men and a Date with Doom." *Miami Herald* (November 8, 1998).

Freidel, David and Linda Schele and Joy Parker. *Maya Cosmos- Three Thousand Years on the Shaman's Path*. New York: William Morrow, 1993.

May, Antoinette. *Passionate Pilgrim: The Extraordinary Life of Alma Reed*. St. Paul: Paragon House Publishers, 1993.

Morely, Sylvanus G. *The Ancient Maya, Third Edition*. Rev: George W. Brainerd. Stanford, Calif: Stanford University Press, 1956.

Peissel, Michel. *The Lost World of Quintana Roo*. New York: E.F. Dutton, 1963.

Perera, Victor and Robert D. Bruce. *The Last Lords of Palenque: The Lacandon Mayas of the Mexican Rain Forest*. Berkeley and Los Angeles: University of California Press, 1982.

Popol Vuh: The Definitive Edition of the Mayan Book of the Dawn of Life. Trans. Dennis Tedlock. New York: Simon & Schuster, 1985.

Recer, Paul. "Study Links Demise of Mayan Civilization to Ancient Dry Spells." *The Associated Press* (March 2003).

Reed, Nelson. *The Caste War of Yucatan*. Standford, Calif: Stanford University Press, 1964.

Reid, Fiona A. *A Field Guide to the Mammals of Central America and Southeast Mexico*. New York: Oxford University Press, 1997.

Stuart, George E. and Gene S. Stuart. *The Mysterious Maya*. National Geographic Society, 1977.

Weiner, Tim. "Mexico's Green Dream: No More Cancuns." *New York Times* (Jan. 14, 2001).

Whitman, George. *The Rag and Bone Shop of the Heart*. Paris, France. Shakespeare & Co., 2000.

Casa Maya

Jeanine Lee Kitchel graduated from Ohio University in 1971 with a double major in Journalism and Comparative Literature. Her travels took her to the West Coast where she worked in Journalism, publishing, and sales in the San Francisco-Bay Area until 1997.

Her ongoing love of Mexico led her to the Yucatan in 1984, and slightly more than a decade later, she left San Francisco for a relaxed lifestyle in Puerto Morelos, a small fishing village on the Quintana Roo coast.

Her *Tales from the Yucatan* travel series can be found on www.planeta.com. She is a contributor to *The Miami Herald, Cancun Edition*, and *Mexico Files*. She divides her time between Puerto Morelos, Mexico, and Haiku, Maui. This is her first book.